j595.76 Patent, Dorothy
P   Hinshaw

         Beetles and how
         they live

DATE			

Beetles
and
How They Live

Dorothy Hinshaw Patent
and Paul C. Schroeder

HOLIDAY HOUSE · NEW YORK

Copyright © 1978 by Dorothy Hinshaw Patent and Paul C. Schroeder
All rights reserved
Printed in the United States of America

Library of Congress Cataloging in Publication Data

Patent, Dorothy Hinshaw.
    Beetles and how they live.

    Includes index.
    SUMMARY: Describes the physiology, habits and
habitats of beetles, their usefulness and harmfulness to
humans, and how to collect them.
        1.   Beetles—Juvenile literature.   [1.   Beetles]
I.   Schroeder, Paul C., joint author.   II.   Title.
QL576.2.P37   595.7′6   78–6725
ISBN 0–8234–0332–7

Contents

This is a Lycid, or net-winged beetle, photographed in Arizona. The fore wings, or elytra, are veined, unlike those of most beetles.

One

What Are Beetles?

It has been said that we live in an "Age of Beetles," and if numbers of the different kinds count for anything, beetles are surely the most important inhabitants of our planet. There are more kinds of them on earth today than of any other sort of animal. This may seem surprising, for the beetles around us are not as obvious as many other creatures. Because of their usually small size and their often secretive habits, we rarely notice them. But they are very important to us and to other living things.

People are familiar with perhaps more beetles than they realize, for many common ones go by inaccurate names. June "bugs" and lady "bugs" are really beetles, as are "fireflies," and "glowworms." And there is the "boll weevil," a serious pest of cotton; it is also a beetle. The common "mealworm," which is used to feed pet frogs and lizards, is actually the larva, or young stage, of a beetle. If you have a garden, you may have seen shiny black ground beetles lumbering across the dirt, or yellow and black flower beetles sitting quietly among the daisies. The fat red larva of the Colorado potato beetle may chew up your potato plants, or bean beetles may damage your garden.

If you live in a damp climate, small flour beetles may infest your kitchen, sharing your packaged nuts and flour with you.

Beetles are, indeed, easy to find and look at, and their variety is enormous. One out of every four species of animal known is a type of beetle. There are more than a quarter of a million kinds of beetles named; some scientists believe that tens of thousands of species remain to be described. Beetles are found almost everywhere—in jungles and meadows, in deserts and ponds. Some are even found along the seashore. There are beetles as small as a pencil dot and beetles larger than a mouse. Many beetles are beautiful, glistening blue and green or brilliant golden in color. Others are rather ugly, with grotesque shapes or with gardens of fungus growing on their backs. In this book we will explore the basic shared characteristics of beetles and the way the extremely successful beetle body is modified for a tremendous variety of life styles.

What Is a Beetle?

Since beetles are insects, they naturally share many characteristics with other insects. They are covered with a tough, protective outer covering which forces them to molt, or shed the old skin, if they are to grow. Like most other insects, beetles do their growing and molting while in a larval stage. Once they become adults, they cease growing altogether. Also like other insects, beetles have a pair of antennae on their heads which are used to sense the environment around them. They have six legs, and their bodies are divided into the same three sections as

A firefly, Apisoma, taking flight. The hard front wings, or elytra, are raised, showing clearly the membranous hind wings below them.

those of other insects—a head, a thorax, and an abdomen. Like most flying insects, beetles have two pairs of wings.

It is usually rather easy, however, to recognize beetles as distinct from other insects. Their modified front wings, which typically cover the rear wings as well as the abdomen, give beetles a rather unusual appearance. These hardened front wings, called elytra (singular, elytron), are probably a factor in the biological success of beetles. The elytra protect the more delicate hind wings and the soft abdomen. Beetles are not easy to kill merely by stepping on them, especially in soft dirt. They are tough, and in addition to making them hard to crush, this toughness enables them to burrow under stones, bark, logs, and into other narrow places. They often live beneath rocks that are difficult for a grown man to move. They can burrow below such heavy obstacles and live in the little protected spaces available where plant roots or smaller stones support the weight of the main rock.

A number of kinds (mainly the rove beetles, family Staphylinidae), however, have short elytra so that the abdomen is exposed. Others such as soldier beetles (family Cantharidae) have soft, flexible elytra which curl up when the animals are preserved. But in most beetles, the elytra are both complete and hard. During evolution some species have completely lost the ability to fly and with it the functional hind wings. The two elytra are fused together (since they no longer need to be opened up to permit use of the hind wings for flight) and the beetle has practically turned into a tank. A number of desert-dwelling darkling beetles (Tenebrionidae) are like this.

The Beetle's Armor

The hard outer covering which protects the beetle so well from the dangers of life is called the cuticle. While all insects have a similar cuticle, beetles have an especially tough one. The cuticle not only acts as a protective outer skin but also serves as an exoskeleton, or outside skeleton. Vertebrates have an endoskeleton; the bones inside our bodies give support and provide attachment places for our muscles. Insects have their skeleton on the outside, but it serves the same functions of support and muscle attachment as does our endoskeleton.

The cuticle is made up of proteins and a chemical called chitin. This is a tough, fibrous material, but it is quite flexible. The cuticle around the joints in an insect's body, legs, and antennae is made up mostly of chitin. The

harder parts of the cuticle are made up of chitin plus proteins, which make it tougher and stronger. Beetle larvae
generally live in protected places and have thinner cuti-
cles than their parents. They shed the old cuticle several
times as they grow, and special cells in the skin secrete a
new, larger cuticle.

The Head of a Beetle

The beetle's head is the first thing to contact changes in
the environment as the beetle moves forward, so the head
contains the most important sense organs, the eyes and the
antennae. Insect eyes are made up of very small units,
each of which takes in a small part of the world around.
Insects such as honeybees and dragonflies, which make
much use of their eyes, have big eyes with many individual units. Other insects, such as many ants that use little
vision in their daily lives, have small eyes with only a few
units. Still other insects, such as some termites, which live
in darkness, are completely blind. Beetles may have large
or small eyes, depending on their way of life. The hunting
tiger beetles have huge eyes, while cave-dwelling beetles
which spend their entire lives in the dark may be completely blind. For most beetles, eyes are used to detect and
avoid their enemies, and the antennae are more important
in finding food and in communicating with other beetles.

The Vital Antennae

The antennae of beetles serve as essential organs of
touch and smell. Beetle antennae come in a great variety
of shapes and sizes and possess special sensory areas and

DR. PHILIP S. CALLAHAN

The antennae of some longhorn beetles have greater length than their bodies; the insects are thought to use them as balancing poles while stepping along narrow twigs.

sensitive hairs. Insect antennae are made up of a long series of segments, usually eleven in beetles. In many, the segments are similar and about the same size. In others, the antennae have become adapted for different functions to suit the different beetle life styles. One of the simplest modifications, elongation, occurs in longhorn beetles (Cerambycidae). In fact, their name derives from the length of the antennae. There are many species of longhorn beetles, some large and colorful. In mounting them for collections, great care must be taken to coil the extremely long antennae above the animal so they do not break off. Some large longhorns are said to use their antennae as balancing poles when crossing narrow twigs, much as a circus acrobat on a tightrope uses a long pole to help keep his or her balance.

In weevils (Curculionidae), a large group of plant-feeding beetles, the antennae are bent at the end of the first segment. Weevils have long snouts, and many of them have a

groove on each side into which the long first segment—
that nearest the body—of each antenna can be tucked.
When the animal folds up its legs and drops from a plant
to avoid a predator, it pulls its antennae into these grooves
as well. The combination of long snout and bent antennae
make it easy to recognize a weevil.

Each antenna of a scarab beetle is also rather odd.
Each of the final three or four segments is extended to-
wards one side. Since the segments are attached to the rest
of the antenna near its end, the final segments resemble a
piece of a comb. The beetle can move the extensions,
spreading them out like combs or pressing them together
so they appear to be solid, clublike endings of the antennae.

Some male glowworms (Phengodidae) have very feath-
ery antennae. Each segment has a pair of branches which

*Among the many shapes of beetle antennae are the lamellate,
or platelike, type, seen on this Magnoculus from South America. When the plates are separated, microscopic sensors on
their surfaces pick up odors.* DR. JAMES E. LLOYD

are much longer than the segment itself. The branches are covered with sensory hairs which make them appear bushy, so that the antennae look something like a household brush. The male uses the many sensory hairs to detect the scent of the female at mating time.

The Rest of the Body

While the beetle's head keeps it in contact with the world through the vital sense organs, the thorax bears the wings and legs. The abdomen contains most of the internal organs. The divisions of the beetle thorax and abdomen are called segments. The thorax has three segments, each of which has a pair of legs. The back two also carry the two pairs of wings. In typical beetles, the two wing-bearing thoracic segments are fused with the abdomen. The first thoracic segment (the prothorax) is separate. Its top portion, the pronotum, forms the obvious middle piece of the typical beetle. It carries the front legs but no wings.

The beetle abdomen has nine segments. But if one tries to count them from the middle to the "tail" end, one can't find that many. On some beetles as few as three are visible; on others as many as eight. One never finds all nine, because the end segments are hidden inside. They are modified differently in males and females and are used in mating. The shapes of these abdominal segments may vary considerably, even between closely related species which look quite similar. They function as a sort of lock-and-key system so that only males of the same species as the female can fit their specially shaped segments into her body during mating. This helps to prevent matings between males and females of different species. Such mechanisms probably help keep populations of closely related beetles separate.

Different Kinds of Legs

The appearance of a beetle's legs tell a lot about the life it leads. Ground beetles (Carabidae), which roam while hunting for prey, have long, thin legs. Burrowers, on the other hand, tend to have short, fat legs, often with stout spines along the edge, which scrape the ground during digging.

Many beetles attempt to escape predators by suddenly clamping all six of their legs tightly to the body and dropping to the ground. The bodies of many kinds with this habit have little niches into which the legs fit when retracted. The beetle thus presents a hard, slippery surface, more like a seed, to such potential predators as succeed in finding them. Pill beetles (Byrrhidae) are perhaps best developed in this way; they can also retract the head deep into the prothorax for further protection. Like many weevils, the pill beetles have special grooves into which they can tuck their antennae.

The legs of some beetles have structures which have nothing to do with walking. Most ground beetles have antenna-cleaners on their front legs. The antenna-cleaner is a notch in the middle section of the leg. It is usually lined with stiff bristles. As the beetle draws its antennae through the notches, the bristles act like combs, removing accumulated dirt. Most ground beetles use spines on the end of the middle legs to clean the combs of the antenna-cleaners. These spines are forced through the bristles on the front leg, thus combing the dirt out of them. It has even been suggested that certain other bristles on the front legs are used in turn for cleaning the comb-cleaners! These are pushed down into the comb-cleaners and the dirt is forced out of them and to the ground. It is obviously important to a ground beetle that its antennae be kept in good condition.

Beetle Respiration

All animals need oxygen for their bodies to function. The hemoglobin in vertebrate blood carries oxygen to the body cells. But insects have a different way of distributing oxygen. The system consists of a network of minute silvery air pipes which lead directly to the tissues, especially the muscles, of the insect, where oxygen is required. This is an interesting and almost unique adaptation in which the oxygen goes straight to the place where it is needed before it dissolves in water. Oxygen can be used by living tissue only when it is dissolved in water. But it can move only slowly through the water (or in this case the insect's body fluids, which are mostly water) without help.

Gases (such as oxygen) can move much more rapidly through other gases (for instance the nitrogen that makes up most of our atmosphere). The insect system of air pipes, called tracheae, allows the oxygen used by the body cells to be rapidly replaced by oxygen from the outside. The waste gas carbon dioxide also can speedily travel to the exterior. The tracheae, as they go more deeply into the body, branch into finer and finer tubules which only at their very ends are filled with fluid. Oxygen must diffuse through the fluid for only a very short distance before reaching the cells within the insect where it is needed.

The presence of these many fluid-filled blind ends, however, is a problem for the insects. Water can evaporate, which means that it moves into a gaseous form. The water can thus be lost almost as readily as the carbon dioxide, and this represents a serious problem for insects which live on dry land and for which finding enough water may be difficult. However, each opening of the tracheal system is covered with a kind of sliding door called a spiracle which opens the tubes to the air only when necessary for getting more oxygen. For instance, when an insect takes flight, its need for oxygen increases dramatically. Its wing muscles must contract rapidly to keep it in the air. This is work, and it requires oxygen. The spiracles open during flight, allowing air to enter.

Strange Habitats

Beetles are found just about everywhere (except in the sea) that living things can survive. There are whole families of them specialized for life in fresh water, and beetles are also among the most successful creatures found in the world's deserts. While some of them can survive the desert's scorching heat, others have found ways to tolerate freezing. Beetles live, in fact, far north into the Arctic, although they are not among the few land animals found so far in Antarctica. Several kinds of ground beetles can survive the winter near Fairbanks, Alaska, where subzero temperatures are common and where the insects would

certainly freeze. Experiments with one such species indicate that this type can withstand freezing only during
the winter. If they are frozen during the summer, they die.
Their secret of winter survival appears to be a built-in
"antifreeze." As winter approaches, the beetles increase
the level of glycerol in their body fluids. This clear, dense
chemical is found in a number of animals which can resist
freezing, although the details of how it works to protect
their bodies from harm are still a bit of a mystery. Summer
beetles lack glycerol, so they are unprotected against the
damaging effects of freezing—largely a matter of cells'
being torn apart by the expansion of the freezing water
in them.

Among the more interesting habitats inhabited by
beetles are caves, which occur extensively in the southeastern United States and in southeastern Europe. In past
ages, some beetles were trapped in caves during changes
in climate (especially during the spread and retreat of
glaciers). They could survive underground on materials
brought into the caves by water and by other organisms.
Once isolated from life above ground, species trapped in
caves evolved in ways which fitted them well for this
life. Such cave creatures tend to be pale and eyeless since
pigment and eyes cost expensive metabolic energy and are
not needed in the dark. They tend to be more sensitive
to odors and vibrations, especially the many small ground
beetles which have become adapted to this sort of an environment.

The lives of cave beetles are interwoven with those of
other cave-dwelling animals. In Mammoth Cave National
Park in Kentucky, one of the most common cave-dwellers

is a cricket. The crickets spend their days on the ceilings of the caves. At night many of them leave and feed upon ants and other insects in the darkness outside the caves. They return to their roosts during daylight. Beneath their roosts, cave-cricket excrement accumulates. This unlikely material provides food for a number of cave animals which can no longer leave the caves, including a blind beetle. Other cave beetles seek out and devour cave cricket eggs, and have long mandibles specialized for just this function.

Beetle Families

Figuring out the relationships among the incredible variety of beetle species is an almost impossible job. Scientists who specialize on beetles (coleopterists) have been working on this enormous task for almost 200 years, and the final results are still not in. Beetles are grouped into many families of related species, but the actual number of families is not yet agreed upon. A recent book on the beetles of the United States lists about 125 families, while another book on beetle classification divides them into 163 families. There is still discussion and wide disagreement on the relationships of beetle families and their appropriate membership. Most of the discussion, however, concerns small groups of relatively unfamiliar beetles. The major kinds have been known for a long time, and it is not difficult to recognize these.

Professional coleopterists must struggle with many subdivisions of beetle families, especially the larger ones. A recent volume on North American members of the weevil family, for example, divided weevils into 42 subfamilies, many of which were further subdivided into "tribes" and "subtribes." While these groupings are important in helping decide which species are most closely related in such large families, they are fortunately of no concern to those of us who study beetles casually.

Naming Beetles

Beetles are named according to a very precise system to which zoologists have agreed through the last century or so. The system is basically the same for all animals, and it dates back to a Swedish botanist whose Latinized name was Carolus Linnaeus. In the eighteenth century, when Linnaeus lived, it was customary to use the Latin language to communicate results in science and in many other fields of learning. The language could be understood by any educated person at that time. Linnaeus devised a system in which each kind of plant and animal would receive a name which could be expressed in two words. Naturally, the words he chose for his descriptions were in Latin, and Latinized scientific names are used for all kinds of living things to this day.

Each particular kind of beetle (or other animal) is identified by two names, a "generic" name followed by a "specific" name, for example *Cicindela oregona,* the Oregon tiger beetle (Latin scientific names are always printed in italics or underlined). The name of the genus, *Cicindela,* occurs in the names of many closely related tiger beetles, said to be in the same genus. Each distinct kind of beetle in the genus has its own second, or species, name, here *oregona.*

Why do we still use such an old system, with words from a language even scientists don't use anymore? The fact is that names in English have been given rather haphazardly to beetles by people who have not studied them. Thus there are May beetles, June beetles, and ladybird beetles. But these names, as people use them, usually refer to several different biological species. Many very similar species of brown scarab beetles are called June beetles, and the name is scientifically useless. Furthermore, the same beetles will have different common names in different languages. Ladybird beetles (or ladybugs), for instance, are known in Germany as *Marienkäfer*, a name which is just as biologically vague as the English "ladybird beetle." "Ladybird" used in England will include pretty much the same species as the term *Marienkäfer*, since England is not far from Germany. But in the United States, many of the species are different, and in Australia, where English is also spoken, the species will be largely different again. But while the name "ladybird" may mean different insects in England, Australia, and the United States, the name *Hippodamia convergens* always refers to the same unique species of ladybird (which we call the "convergent lady beetle"). A scientist in England, Germany, Russia, or anywhere else will know exactly which beetle species is referred to by that scientific name.

The Latin names may seem strange to speakers of English. But if detailed names were invented for each species in English, they would still have to be memorized and used as foreign words by zoologists in other countries, for whom English is a foreign language. So too for us, names in German would be as difficult and foreign as those in Latin, perhaps more so. Scientists have agreed to use the Latin names because they have a long history, are equally accessible to all, and because they may be readily traced in the literature of zoology. There is really no reason to change them, since they are well established and used throughout the world.

There are still many species of beetles which have not been recognized, and hundreds of new ones are described and named each year. These new species are often discovered, not by difficult expeditions to inaccessible places, but in unstudied collections in museums, where they have been sitting for decades waiting for the right person to come along and examine them and to recognize them as new. With so many kinds of beetles, no one person can master them all, and the work of naming the new ones falls to the small number of people who specialize in specific families or even subfamilies, and who try to figure out the relationships between all the species known in a given group. Only such people can recognize the small differences which often turn out to indicate a separate species.

Two
Beetle Foods and Feeding

The mouthparts of some insects are specialized for feeding on a specific type of food. Butterflies, for example, specialize in drinking the liquid nectar found in flowers and have mouthparts modified into a sort of flexible drinking straw which permits them to suck up the nectar very efficiently. The mouthparts of beetles, however, are usually little modified from the basic chewing type from which all insect variations are thought to have evolved. There is a pair of mandibles (jaws) which move from side to side like scissors.

These are the most obvious mouthparts. They move in and out of a boxlike chamber which is formed in front of the mouth itself by an upper "lip" above and a lower "lip" below. Both "lips" are really hard, flattened, platelike structures which form the top and bottom of the "box." There is also a pair of accessory jaws just beneath the mandibles which close when the mandibles open and vice-versa. They help the beetle to avoid dropping the food it is chewing. Since the basic movement of the mouthparts is from side to side rather than the familiar up-and-down sort of chewing we practice ourselves, it is at first a bit bewildering to try to understand what is going on when one watches a beetle eating. There are a lot of moving parts.

Most beetles feed this way, although there are some exceptions. For example, one group of blister beetles (Meloidae) has specialized in feeding on flowers much as butterflies have, and these have elongated mouthparts which, while not as spectacular as those of butterflies, probably work in a similar fashion. The mandibles have been lost in a few beetles and have become very exaggerated in others. Male stag beetles (Lucanidae), for example, have huge mandibles that are used for fighting and are useless in feeding.

Beetle Digestion

When a beetle eats, the food passes from the mouthparts to the front portion of the gut, which is lined with chitin, rather like the outside of the animal but thinner and more flexible. In general, there are differences between the structure of the gut in carnivores—meat-eaters —which must accommodate large meals at irregular and frequently long intervals, and in herbivores—plant-eaters —which tend to send smaller volumes of food through the digestive tract at a more steady rate. The carnivores have a roomy crop where the bulk of the prey can be stored while waiting to move on down the line for digestion. Then the food passes into a muscular tube called the gizzard, which serves to crush the food (it is not really well chewed at the time it is eaten). The gizzard is frequently armed with stiff hairs which serve to filter material leaving it. Only the particles small enough to pass through go further into the digestive chamber. Larger pieces are retained for further grinding.

The digestive region is called the midgut. It is relatively thin-walled and flexible. It is protected on the inside by a thin membrane which is secreted at its front end. This "peritrophic membrane" wraps up the food bundles yet permits chemical exchange to take place so that the insect can absorb the nutrients released from the food by its digestive enzymes. The remains of the food, still wrapped in the peritrophic membrane, then pass into the hindgut, where water is taken from it for the body's needs.

The junction of the midgut and the hindgut is easy to see under a microscope since just there a group of tubules joins the digestive tract. These serve not digestion but the elimination of metabolic waste products. They are named after the Italian anatomist who first described them in the seventeenth century: the Malpighian tubules. They act somewhat the way the human kidney does in that they filter the contents of the body cavity the way a portion of the kidney filters blood. This filtered fluid, which contains metabolic wastes, is dumped into the intestine at the point where it meets the hindgut, and water is salvaged from it. Most insects live on land and usually must conserve their water supply. Thus both digestive and metabolic wastes pass through the hindgut, which specializes in recovering much of the water that would otherwise be lost when they are eliminated from the body.

What Beetles Eat

As we have seen, the variety of beetle life is tremendous. So it is not very surprising that almost every possible food source is used by some kind of beetle. We can make a fairly easy distinction between beetles that eat animals and those that eat plants. Within these types we can distinguish between generalists, which accept a wide variety of food items, and specialists, which can eat only one kind of plant or one type of animal food. The destructive Japanese beetle, which eats all sorts of plants, is a generalist, while the cave beetles which eat only cricket eggs are extreme specialists.

Beetle larvae are very different from the adults and often require a different food. The larvae may specialize in one kind of food while adults may feed on something totally different. Then larvae and adults do not compete with one another. This is thought to be a major advantage of the type of life cycle beetles have, which involves a complete metamorphosis from a wormlike larva to a typical (and very different) adult. The beetles share this advantage with other insect groups in which such metamorphosis takes place, such as butterflies and flies. If the two food sources are completely unrelated to one another (as with the flower-feeding adults of species with wood-eating larvae), the beetles can live only in places where the supply of both food types is assured at the proper time of year.

Not all beetles have different larval and adult foods,

however. Beetles which specialize in a single food plant, such as many weevils and leaf beetles, tend to use that plant both as larvae and as adults. Humans have on occasion put this type of narrow specialization to good use. Saint John's wort, called Klamath weed in this country, is an especially undesirable plant which came to the United States from Europe. It grows fast and strong, replacing nutritious native grasses wherever it gets established. Animals which eat Klamath weed develop sore mouths and scabby skins. They do not thrive. Like many introduced plants, this weed was able to take over so easily because it had no natural enemies here. Scientists found a pea-sized, purplish-green leaf beetle which would eat only this unwanted weed. When introduced into the United States to combat St. John's wort, this beetle did such a good job that within a few years the weed was under control and native grasses were again growing in the pastures.

Plant-Eaters

Plant-feeders have specialized in almost every conceivable way to utilize all portions of different plants. Many chew leaves directly. Larvae of others mine leaves and stems (especially leaf beetles—Chrysomelidae). They chew their way along the inside of the leaf, tunneling through the substance between its two surfaces. Leaves may be eaten by taking bites from the edges or by eating small holes in the middle. Particular kinds of beetles tend to do one or the other. Some adult weevils cut leaves and roll up the pieces to provide a protected feeding place for their larvae. Although most flower-visiting beetles feed on nectar and pollen, some, such as the green June beetle, consume the petals as if they were leaves.

Other members of the plant-eating families, such as bean weevils (Bruchidae), specialize in eating seeds. Some true weevils also live in seeds and even in those larger seeds we call nuts. Some weevils (like Curculio) have a very elongated snout which they use to excavate holes in nuts such as acorns. They lay their eggs in this cavity. The larva need only hatch and start chewing, since it is surrounded by food.

Plant roots are also used by many kinds of beetles, primarily as a larval food. Three families are prominent in the list of root-feeders. They include the larvae of click beetles, called wireworms (Elateridae), and larvae of both scarabs and weevils. Some of these are destructive to cultivated plants. They feed on roots of plants as varied as golf-green grass and strawberries.

Many beetles feed on the woody parts of plants—bark, stems, and even the hearts of tree trunks, both living and decaying. Tiny bark beetles (Scolytidae) attack sick or dying trees (they sometimes invade healthy trees too) and feed upon the succulent layers of living tissue which lie just beneath the bark. Successful penetration of a tree by a single individual results in the release of chemicals into the air (from both the tree and the beetle) which may attract hordes of beetles. These start boring soon after they arrive, often resulting in serious damage to the tree. If you have ever stripped the bark from a log, you have probably seen the tunnels made by bark beetle larvae as they move away from the cavity which the female ex-

A heavy infestation of bark beetles can produce fantastic patterns beneath tree bark, such as this, the work of the Douglas fir beetle.

cavated to lay her eggs. In many species, each larva bores its own tunnel as it grows. The beetles are frequently called engraver beetles because of the interesting patterns these tunnels produce under the bark.

Partners with Fungi

Some bark beetles are called ambrosia beetles. These usually very small beetles bore narrow galleries deep into the wood. They use the galleries as nurseries for a fungus which they carry with them from tree to tree. Many species even have small cavities in their bodies specially adapted to carry the fungus spores, which they "plant" in new galleries. They do not eat the tree itself but use it to sustain their own specialized food. The fungus develops best when secretions provided by the beetle are present to nourish it and keep down the growth of competing "weed" fungi. The fungi probably provide the insects with vitamins which would be unavailable in a diet of pure wood. They are absolutely necessary to the ambrosia beetles. However, many other bark beetles carry fungi with them which they use to permit greater growth and survival when conditions are poor. These bark beetles do the most damage to our forests, for their fungi are capable of living without the beetles, just as the beetles can live without the fungi. But the fungus is not good for the tree, and eventually fungi growing in many beetle galleries can kill a large tree. Fungi such as that responsible for Dutch-elm disease, which has killed most of the elm trees in North America, are transmitted in this manner by a bark beetle attracted to elms.

Dead-Wood Feeders

Once a tree has been weakened by bark beetles or has been overtaken by any of the other fates which might befall it, it becomes a complex environment for a host of different insects. Such communities are dominated by beetles. Fallen logs, whether freshly cut or old and decayed, are excellent places to hunt for different and unusual beetles. A fresh log may be attacked by round- or flat-headed wood-borers (larvae of longhorn beetles and metallic wood-boring beetles) which are specialized for this sort of life. The log is usually invaded at the same time by fungi which start the process of breaking up the wood. With time the formerly tight bark loosens slightly, allowing space for members of the "under bark" group. These eat other insects and are there to prey upon the wood-eating larvae. The common North American flat bark beetle is bright red. This beetle is so remarkably flat that it fits easily into very narrow spaces beneath bark, where it spends most of its time.

There are hard bracket fungi which appear on the trunks of dead and even some living trees. These, too, have their associated beetles, notably a whole family of especially small ones called minute tree fungus beetles. In the eastern United States, larger beetles with a warty appearance and horns in front also inhabit bracket fungi. These relatives of the mealworm beetle are specialized for life on the fungi. They eat the fungus spores, lay their eggs in the fungi, and may stay with their own "home" fungus for several years. Other mealworm relatives live beneath bark, where they probably feed on small fungi growing in that moist, protected atmosphere. Some handsomely marked beetles feed on fungi as well, such as the pleasing fungus beetles. These are especially abundant and colorful in humid tropical forests, where fungi are abundant.

Digesting Wood

The consumption of dead wood by insects is an interesting biological phenomenon. Most animals cannot digest cellulose, the principal material remaining in a dead log. A number of insect types have nonetheless specialized in eating wood. The best known of these are the termites.

These insects cannot digest wood themselves, although they eat large quantities of it. The actual digestion is performed in the gut of the termite by a remarkable collection of complex protozoans, very small single-celled animals which are specialized for life in the gut of the termites and without which the termites cannot survive.

Some beetles can do what termites themselves cannot. Round-headed wood-borers (larvae of longhorn beetles) are able to digest cellulose without relying on small inhabitants of their digestive tract to do the job for them. They also benefit from food materials which the tree transports through the small vessels which make up the wood, and of which traces remain. Some round-headed wood-borers are specialized for the wood from particular types of trees, while others accept a great variety of different kinds. As one might expect, the second type includes the more abundant, easy-to-find species. In tropical rain forests there are many kinds of trees, but not many of a given kind. Correspondingly, there are a great many species of longhorn beetles, but individuals of most species are encountered relatively seldom.

Once they have started their development, the larvae of some wood-eaters survive for a long time, slowly gnawing their way along. If the wood is poor in nutrients, they may take years to develop. They may come out long after someone has used the seasoned lumber in construction or furniture-building. Beetles have emerged from furniture and house timbers 20 and even 30 years after construction. In some of these cases, the larvae were probably alive in the wood all this time. When furniture is made from tropical hardwoods imported from exotic places like the

Philippine Islands, interesting beetles, quite unfamiliar even to local entomologists, may make a surprise appearance. Records of such occasional "imports" are quite frequent in cities where ships arrive from faraway places and are unloaded.

Some beetles can bore through exceedingly hard wood, and some have even been known to move from the wood of a pole carrying electric transmission wires right on through the lead sheathing which protects the wires. Such activity leaves holes through which water can get in and cause short circuits, resulting in power failures. Such beetles have been called "lead cable borers" or "short-circuit beetles."

Thriving on Decay

Logs which have been on the ground for a number of years, especially where the climate is reasonably moist, tend to disintegrate into small chunks which can be separated with the hand. This level of decay is produced largely by the activities of bacteria and fungi. Trees in this condition provide the habitat for still another group of beetles, the larvae of which probably subsist more on the bacteria and fungi than on the wood itself. These include some of the largest and most interesting beetles, the stag beetles and the large scarabs.

Another interesting type of older, decaying wood is driftwood, which typically floats for a fairly long time in ocean or lake. It becomes water-soaked and is then washed up on a beach. Such a long bath in the ocean kills many of the organisms, including the bacteria and fungi, which are

the normal inhabitants of dead wood. But some beetles
(as some false blister beetles—Oedemeridae) have managed to make use of this wood as a larval habitat, although
how they do it is not well understood. Adults of these
beetles may be found under logs washed up high on the
beach or crawling on them at night. They are occasionally
attracted to lights located near a beach. But they are not
very abundant, even where conditions appear right for
them.

Predators

So far we have discussed beetles which feed on plants,
often specializing in particular plant species or particular
parts of their favorite kinds. But many species of beetles
eat other animals, even other beetles. Predatory beetles
tend to be fast-moving creatures which are active, and
hence visible, while they hunt. Many land beetles and
most of the larger aquatic beetles feed on other animals.
Both adults and larvae of large diving beetles can catch
and eat small fish. The larvae are often called "water
tigers." They inject digestive juices into a captured fish
through holes at the tips of the jaws and suck out the
resulting broth. They do not chew up and swallow the fish
itself. It is obviously unwise to keep water beetles in an
aquarium with small fish.

Ground beetles (Carabidae) are active, usually black
beetles which are common under stones and boards almost
anywhere in the northern hemisphere. Most of them wander about seeking their victims at night and hide during
the day. Some of the most formidable predators are very

specialized ground beetles called tiger beetles. The North American species all look rather similar—the head with bulging eyes and crossed, sickle-shaped jaws. The elytra are rather square in outline and range from dark indigo to brilliant green by way of iridescent purple, all with white swirls in characteristic patterns.

The attractive appearance of these saber-tooths of the insect world makes them great favorites with collectors. (There is even a magazine devoted only to this group.) Tiger beetles all have excellent eyesight and can run and fly very rapidly. They are the most agile of beetles and, in their favorite habitat—a sunny spot in the open on the sand—they can be quite difficult to capture. After a collector gets one, he or she has to remember those sharp jaws, for the beetle won't hesitate to bite in defense and can deliver a memorable nip. The pursuit of tiger beetles in the sun is probably as close as beetle-collecting comes to being a real sport. Tiger beetles use their large, prominent eyes to spot prey up to several inches away (a long distance for an insect). They can run fast enough to cover a distance of a few inches in less than a second, giving their victims very little getaway time.

The tiger beetles, with their dazzling speed and powerful jaws, stand in great contrast to the familiar slow and plump-bodied ladybird beetles, most of which are specialized to feed upon aphids and scale insects. Aphids are minute soft-bodied insects which stick a long "nose" (really modified mouthparts) into the stems and leaf ribs of green plants and feed on the nutrient fluids which flow through them. They are thus sort of tethered by their "noses"; they are not free to move rapidly out of the way

This ladybird beetle is feeding on a Norway maple aphid, another of which is seen to its right.

of a predator. With such fixed victims, ladybird beetles can afford to be leisurely predators. They need not be built for speed or power. In fact, they resemble the leaf beetles, plant-feeders which live in similar places. Ladybird beetles and their active larvae thus graze on aphids much as cattle might graze upon immobile blades of grass. Scale insects, the other major prey of common ladybird beetles, are even more sluggish than aphids. Since both aphids and scale insects damage garden plants, the ladybird beetles are regarded as friends of the gardener.

Specialized Hunters

Tiger beetles and most other ground beetles are willing to eat almost any prey they may find. The ladybird beetles are limited in their feeding habits, but some beetles are still more specialized in their choice of prey, such as the larvae of soft-winged beetles (Phengodidae). These are known as banded glowworms because the larvae can give off light. They are specialized to feed upon millipedes, the slow animals known as "thousand-leggers." These beetles are closely related to fireflies. Banded glowworms are elongated, wormlike creatures which will attack almost any kind of millipede. These slowly moving, many-legged animals offer little resistance and cannot run away. The glowworm larva hops aboard the moving millipede like the hero in a western movie hopping onto a train to work his way forward over the tops of the cars to the locomotive. The larva also goes forward until it is in a position to bite into the "neck" of the millipede, where the thousand-legger's armor protects it least. The bite severs a nerve and paralyzes the millipede. The larva then usually buries the millipede, snips off the head, and enters the long tubular body from the front, where it begins to feed. Only the larvae feed in this way; the adults do not seem to feed at all.

Another type of ground beetle can also serve as an example of a specialized predator, this time on snails and slugs. These beetles have long, rather thin heads with prominent mandibles. The pronotum is also rather thin and elongated. This peculiar shape seems well adapted for allowing the predator to force its mouthparts well back into the shell of a snail it is eating. Some species feed upon slugs, which lack shells. They are probably descended from species which did eat snails. This could explain their having a shape which no longer seems required for their more recent slug-eating habits.

Other predatory beetles are not specialized in body form, but they occur in specific habitats where particular types of prey are found. Rove beetles live in places where large numbers of fly larvae—maggots—are to be expected. Certain rove beetles are associated with animal droppings, or dung, to which many flies are attracted. The flies come there to reproduce. They lay their eggs on the dung, which provides food for their young. The beetles are there to prey upon the soft, defenseless, and abundant maggots. Along the beaches of the West Coast there is another situation in which fly reproduction is obvious and abundant. Kelp flies rise in clouds from large dead seaweeds which have washed high up on the beach and started to decay. A characteristic group of rove beetles is present under the kelp to feast upon the high fly population (this time the maggots live in the rotting plant material). In both of these situations one may also come upon the curious barrel-shaped hister beetles which feed upon the fly larvae as well.

Three
Wings and Flight

One secret of insect success is the ability to fly. This capacity developed long ago, fairly early in the history of insects and long before there were birds. Flying has been very important in making insects the dominant animals (in terms of sheer numbers) that they are in the world today. At the time they developed wings, no other kind of animal could fly. In the air there was no competition.

The wings of insects developed from flaps on the top of the back which were at first useful in gliding. Their wings are not modified legs; rather they are unique structures not represented at all in the anatomy of crayfish or spiders, which are otherwise rather similar to insects. In the insects we know today we can distinguish the slow flight of dragonflies and butterflies from the fast flight of bees and flies. The main difference between these two types is the number of times the wings move per second. Bees and flies beat their wings much faster than dragonflies and butterflies. These two groups of insects have developed interesting differences related to their kind of flight.

Oddly enough, the beetles belong in the group with bees and flies, despite the fact that they usually fly rather slowly, even clumsily. In fact, the wing-beat frequency in large beetles like big scarabs is probably lower than in some dragonflies. Scientists think that the mechanism for producing high wing-beat frequency developed to meet the needs of small flying insects whose evolutionary descendants have inherited their superior flight mechanism. It was also well suited for competition with larger flying insects, so that now there are both small and large insects with the "newer" type of flight.

To understand how beetles fly we must consider the way insects move their wings, a process which is different from what one might assume. In most insects, movement of the wings is indirect. The muscle which contracts to move the wing is not actually attached to it. Instead, one end attaches to a spot on the wall of the thoracic segment bearing the wings; the other attaches to the top of the same segment. Both ends of the muscle are anchored to pieces of the exoskeleton called plates. Movement of one of these plates puts pressure on the base of the wing which either lifts or lowers it.

The pair of muscles which runs from front to back beneath the top of the thorax (called the notum) shortens and makes the notum pop into a convex dome shape. This causes the wings to go down because of the complicated way the wings are attached to the sides of the thorax, just beneath the notum. When the muscles which run from top to bottom shorten, they tend to flatten the dome. This causes the wings to go up. The muscles take turns contracting in very rapid succession, too fast for one to see the top of the thorax bulging out and flattening again, even if there were a way to hold the flying beetle still.

Flight muscles in insects must contract rapidly for efficient flight. One reason that they can contract so often is that they do not shorten very much each time. Many muscles contract until they are perhaps three-quarters of their relaxed length. But flight muscles after contraction are almost the same length they were before. They have to be measured carefully to see the small difference.

The reason for this lies in the way the wings are attached to the body. Think of the wing of a beetle as if it were the board of a seesaw. The board of the seesaw is supported in the middle. But the supporting structure of the beetle wing is not placed in the middle. It is very near the end of the wing that is closer to the body. This end reaches over the side plate of the beetle's body just a little bit, so the beetle wing is like a seesaw in which the board is pushed almost all the way across the central support. One would have to pull very hard on the short end of such a seesaw to make the long end rise up in the air. But one would not have to pull the short end down very far. Since this is the way beetle wings are made, beetle flight muscles must be very strong, but they do not have to move very far. Because they contract so little, each cycle of contraction and relaxation can take a very short time, and the wings can beat very fast.

Getting Enough Oxygen

Flight muscles are able to contract many more times in a second (well over a hundred times a second in many flying insects) than more typical muscles in, say, the leg. This means that these muscles use a lot of energy, so they need a lot of oxygen, and flight muscles are usually provided with an extra-large supply of air. In beetles this is accomplished in two different ways. Some, like the large scarab beetles, have sizable air sacs in the segment with the flight muscles; these can store fairly large volumes of air. Before, during, and after flight, this air is forcibly replaced with fresh air by a strong pumping of the abdomen. This compresses and expands the thorax, forcing air to move through it. This process is called ventilation, a term also used to describe our own breathing. The old air in our lungs is replaced at least partially by fresh air each time we breathe.

In other beetles, an interesting system has developed which uses the forward movement of the flying beetle to force air at high speed through especially large tracheae in the thorax. These open at both the front and back of the thorax. As the beetle starts to fly, air rushes into the spiracle in front and pushes out the stale air, which leaves by the hind opening. As long as the beetle is flying, fresh air streams through the thorax past the wing muscles. The flow stops only when the beetle stops flying, when the flight muscles also stop needing so much oxygen.

Another interesting feature of the flight muscles is the fact that they do not need constant nerve stimulation to cause them to contract continuously. Once a nerve has stimulated the first muscle contraction, the flight muscles contract in response to the slight stretch which they undergo when the opposing set of muscles contracts. The stretch sets off an electrical discharge of the muscle cells just as a nerve does, causing it to contract. This makes them different from most muscles, which must be stimulated directly by a nerve each time.

Although the stimulation of a muscle by a nerve is electrical, and to our way of thinking, very rapid, it does take time, usually about one one-hundredth of a second. This means that in a second, a nerve could stimulate a muscle to contract no more than about a hundred times. Faster wing-beat frequencies, which are common in small flies and mosquitoes, would be impossible with such a system. The muscle has become independent of the nerve in fast-flying insects. In this way, the time taken getting the message from the nerve cell to the muscle, and then for recharging the nerve cell, can be saved. With adequate supplies of oxygen and food, the muscles themselves have the capacity to contract 200 and even 300 times per second.

Warming Up

When a large beetle stops flying and folds its wings beneath its elytra, the wings become separated from the action of the flight muscles. Therefore, if the muscles contract when the wings are folded, the wings do not move. The anatomy of this system is complex, but the reason for it is fairly simple. Although we tend to think of insects as "cold-blooded" animals, the flight muscles work best at a temperature of about 100° F (38° C). When a beetle wants to take flight on a cooler day, it must warm up. The means by which this is accomplished are similar to warming up a car engine on a cold day—the heat produced by the engine itself while the car remains in neutral makes the engine warmer, so that it functions better. When a suitable warm temperature has been reached, the car may be put into gear and driven away. The beetle also uses the heat generated by its engine, the flight muscle itself, to raise the temperature in the thorax. The rapid contraction of these powerful muscles also generates heat.

After a suitable period of such warmup (how long depends on the outside temperature and how active the beetle has been in the previous few minutes), the wings are extended and at the same time the flight mechanism is put "in gear." Now the muscles will move the wings when they contract. Large beetles also can walk and run better when the body temperature is higher than about 85° F (29.5° C). When such beetles are forced to walk or turn themselves over from being on their backs, they will raise their body temperature by working the flight muscles as if preparing to fly. If one touches a beetle when this is happening, one can feel the vibration of the thorax. Beetles can thus use their flight muscles to generate heat which will make other muscles, like those associated with walking, work better, even when they don't fly.

The Elytra in Flight

When we talk about flight in insects, we must remember that in beetles the front pair of wings has been transformed into the tough wing covers called elytra. Since these are not used for flying, there are no flight muscles in the body near where they are attached. In other insects which have only one set of flight muscles it is the front, not the rear, set which remains. A flying beetle must lift its elytra high enough to allow the wings beneath to unfold and to beat without interference. They are not moved much in flight, although they probably do provide some

The elytra of a beetle are usually raised well above the hind wings for flight; a few species lift them only slightly, however. This is the firefly Photinus tanytoxus.

of the "lift" which keeps the beetle in the air. Scarabs fly poorly with their elytra removed, so even though they do not beat, the elytra do contribute to the success and efficiency of flight. Their main value may be to improve flying stability.

A few beetles fly with their elytra lifted only slightly from their backs rather than stretched out on each side. Adults of a metallic wood-boring beetle are frequently found on flowers in the southern part of the United States. When these beetles fly, their wings protrude through small notches in the sides of the elytra, and the elytra are kept locked together by a tongue-and-groove mechanism. Such beetles are often colored yellow and black, usually in a striped pattern with most of the color on the elytra. Since they spend much of their time feeding on flowers, it is thought that the color pattern is an imitation of bees and wasps which also visit flowers. By flying with the elytra in almost their resting position, the beetles resemble bees or wasps as well when flying as when at rest. In mimicking animals which birds are reluctant to attack, these beetles maintain their beelike look even while in the air.

Beetles That Cannot Fly

There are other interesting variations in the wings of beetles. Populations of many kinds of ground beetles include individuals with short wings as well as others with wings of the usual length. Some populations even include wingless individuals, which certainly cannot fly at all. The short-winged forms cannot fly either, and it would appear that since the wingless ones survive, it is not critical for these ground beetles to be able to fly in order to survive and reproduce.

It used to be thought that the wingless forms would tend to develop in places where flying insects would be blown away from their natural habitat, especially islands and mountain tops. This idea has been examined carefully with respect to the ground beetles, and it has been found that it is probably not correct, even though it seems very logical. The islands which had been studied in making this assumption were mountainous islands, which do have a lot of wingless forms. Many mountain-top areas do, too, and it has since been realized that the wingless forms on those islands are probably there because of the mountains, not because they happen to be on islands. Low, fairly flat islands, even if they are fairly windy, have mostly species that can fly. These beetles probably fly only on days when conditions are favorable for them, and thus avoid being blown out to sea by staying home when the weather is dangerous.

The reason that such short-winged and wingless forms tend to concentrate on mountain tops is less well understood. One theory is that wings are mainly good for permitting a beetle to find suitable new areas fairly close by, especially in places where many kinds of ground beetles compete for space and food. On mountain tops there are fewer species and the individuals are already in the only available habitat. Perhaps they no longer need to fly for purposes of dispersal. When "defective" beetles with short or even absent wings develop, they can still survive as a population over the long term. It is known from breeding experiments that a simple genetic change can produce winglessness. One large wingless ground beetle from South Africa was recently found to still have muscles equivalent to the flight muscles of flying forms, but without the special structure usually associated with beetle flight muscles. Under the electron microscope, its muscles looked more like the typical slow muscles found in dragonflies.

Miniature Beetles

The tiny feather-winged beetles (Ptiliidae) have very peculiar wings. These beetles are only from one-fourth to one millimeter long, and probably feed on fungi. But it is their peculiar "feather wing" which makes them unique. The wings do not resemble typical insect wings, but rather look like narrow pegs sticking out from each side of the beetle. Along each edge and around the tip of the "peg" is a thin row of long hairs which cover somewhat the same area that a typical wing would cover. Not much is known about how these wings work, but such wings are also found in very small wasps and flies. It is thought that they are related to the small size of all these insects. The feather-wing may serve its owner as a sort of miniature hang-glider. When the wings are spread, the air will pick up the beetle and carry it like a dandelion seed to a new, unplanned destination. It may be that air is too dense for minute wings of normal shape to work properly, especially since such a small beetle would not have much space in its thorax for bulky flight muscles. Perhaps these beetles can gain one of the main benefits of flight, dispersal, by hang-gliding just as well as by flying.

Four

How Beetles Reproduce

Because beetles have so many different life styles, they have a variety of approaches to continuing their species. Some beetles, such as ladybirds, reproduce rapidly and may have several generations in one year. Others have just one generation each season, and a few have life cycles which take two or more years. The larvae of each species are adapted for their own special way of life just as much as the adults are. The amount of care the adults take in assuring the survival of the next generation varies, too, from oil beetles which merely lay their eggs loosely in the soil to sexton beetles which feed and protect their larvae.

The males and females of a great many beetles look almost identical from the outside, but some kinds have obvious differences. One sex may be larger than the other. Male longhorn beetles are often smaller than the female, while female stag and scarab beetles (Scarabaeidae) are frequently smaller than their horned mates. The enlarged horns or mandibles of these male beetles can be an impressive sight. The elephant beetle male has four big horns, while the male hercules beetle (one of the longest insects) has a horn which is almost half the length of his whole body. This makes him appear huge in comparison to his hornless mate. Male stag beetles have gigantic mandibles which appear to be used to fight other males and to hold onto the female during mating. Some of these huge scarabs, such as the atlas beetle, have bright metallic colors in addition to their huge horns; the females are plain and dull.

Sometimes the male has a more "normal" beetle appearance while the female is the different-looking one. Female weevils often have longer snouts than the males; they use these to drill holes in hard nuts or seeds as nests for the young before laying their eggs. One strange feature of beetles from several families is the "larviform" female. "Larviform" means just what it seems to—"having the shape of the larva." Such female beetles never develop the beetle body shape. Instead, they are long, wingless, and usually not very active. They are able to mate and lay eggs, however, so they are truly fully mature females.

Finding a Mate

With a few spectacular exceptions, such as fireflies, most beetles find their mates either by apparent random encounters while hunting for food or by use of chemical sex attractants. Ground beetles which roam around hunting for food may encounter one another in their wanderings and pair up, while dung beetles can easily find mates which are attracted to the same fresh dung heap. Most beetles, however, require a more foolproof means of locating a member of the opposite sex that is ready to mate, and the great majority of beetles appear to advertise themselves chemically.

A pair of mealworm beetles, Tenebrio molitor, *mating. Below, the male attempts to mate with a glass rod dipped in a solution of the female's sex-attractant pheromone.*

Usually it is the female which produces the sex attractant, called a pheromone. Chemical communication is actually very common in insects—pheromones exist which aid in following ant trails and spreading alarm among bees and ants as well as for attracting the opposite sex. A female beetle ready to mate releases her sex attractant from glands on her abdomen. The powerful chemicals are carried on the wind. If a male of her kind ready to mate catches her scent, he will fly into the wind and search out the source of the odor.

Bark Beetle Attractants

Chemical communication is a very efficient means of bringing together small flying animals which are spread out over a wide area. This can be seen especially well in the bark beetles. In order to overcome the defenses of a living tree, bark beetles need to attack in large numbers. But they do not ordinarily remain together except when attacking a tree, so they must be gathered together somehow at the right time and place. Each bark beetle species has its own pheromone system to accomplish this feat. Sometimes the males hunt first for the trees and attract females with their scent, and sometimes the females do the initial searching and attracting.

The unmated female elm bark beetle, which carries the deadly Dutch elm disease, produces an attractant pheromone consisting of three different chemical substances while she is boring into an elm tree. This pheromone mixture attracts both male and female elm bark beetles to the tree, and they join in the attack. The male beetles mate with the females. Once they have mated, the females no longer produce the attractant. This makes an effective self-limiting system. At first, many males and females are attracted by the combined pheromone from all the unmated females. These insects work on the tree together, breaking down its defenses. When all the females have mated and are ready to lay their eggs, however, the attraction ceases and they can go on with the business of egg-laying without competition from more beetles.

The Douglas fir beetle is one of the few beetles known to use sound as part of its communication system. The female Douglas fir beetle releases an attractive pheromone which brings the male. When he arrives at the entrance to the gallery she has bored in the wood, he announces himself with a special sound. This sound has an immediate effect on the female; she ceases at once to release her attractant, and no more males will come to call. The special sound-producer consists of a "strummer" near the end of the male's abdomen which is stroked along a file of parallel ridges on the underside of his left elytron. Communication among beetles with such soft, short-range sounds may be more common than is yet realized.

Mating

Once they have found each other, the male and female beetle mate. All land animals share the same problem—how to get the male sperms to the female egg without either drying out. The almost universal solution is internal fertilization; the male transfers sperms directly into the body of the female with a special organ. The male beetle has a structure at the end of the abdomen called the aedeagus. Most of the time the aedeagus is pulled into the telescoped final abdominal segments of the male's body. But at mating time the aedeagus is extended and placed inside an opening into the reproductive tract of the female. Sperms travel through a duct in the aedeagus into the body of the female. Female beetles do not lay their eggs immediately after mating. Instead, they store the sperms in special sacs connected to their reproductive tract. The sperms are released from the sacs as the eggs are laid and fertilization then can take place.

The Beetle Egg

Because they are exposed to the air, beetle eggs must be protected from drying out. They have a special outer covering called the chorion which helps hold in moisture. The chorion is produced right inside the ovary and is applied to the egg there. This leads to problems in fertilization, for the sperms must be able to penetrate the egg despite its tough outer shell. Insect eggs have minute holes in the chorions through which the sperms can swim and fertilize them. These "micropyles" are extremely narrow passageways, but insect sperms are especially long and thin, and so can squeeze through.

Insect eggs in general are quite large, for they contain a generous amount of yolk that nourishes the developing embryos. The large insect egg can be a problem for the especially small kinds of beetles. Some featherwing females are so small that one egg is just about half the length of the entire body. Needless to say, these insects can mature only one egg at a time.

Most female beetles lay the eggs in some protected spot, often near or right on the larval food. Leaf-eating beetles lay the eggs glued to the underside of food-plant leaves. The larvae do not have to travel in order to begin eating. A female weevil lays her eggs directly inside the food after drilling the cavity with her strong snout, while bark beetle females may bore out elaborate tunnels with little niches in the walls for the eggs. Many water beetles produce fancy cocoons that protect their eggs from drowning. The great silver water beetle female weaves silk around her egg mass and attaches it to a floating twig or leaf. At one end of this cocoon is a "periscope" which sticks up out of the water and may help ensure an adequate air supply for the developing embryos. Some other water beetles actually carry their cocoons around with them.

The number of eggs laid by any beetle species depends on the amount of care which they are given. The oil beetles, which merely deposit the eggs in the soil, may produce thousands of eggs, while dung beetles, which gather food for their larvae and carefully bury it, may lay fewer than a half dozen eggs. In some beetles, the effort of the female is put into the preparation of a protected place for her offspring to develop, while in others her effort is the physiological one involved in making enough high-energy yolk for hundreds or thousands of eggs.

The Beetle Larva

When a beetle larva is ready to hatch, it must break through the tough chorion which has protected it up to now. Many beetle larvae have special "hatching spines" to aid them. Some of the spines are used to cut through the chorion while others are pressed against the sides of the egg while the larva struggles to free itself. Often the mandibles are used to bite a hole in the chorion, too.

Whatever their specialized life style, many beetle larvae share certain traits such as a hard head, three thoracic segments, and eight or nine abdominal segments. It usually has biting mouthparts like the adults, but often they are somewhat simpler in structure. Most beetle larvae also have simple eyes and antennae. Active, hunting larvae have strong, well-developed legs and a tough body to match. Some hunters even have feelers on their rear ends and can turn the end of the abdomen under as an extra leg to hold up the long body. Tiger beetle larvae are hunters, but they live in burrows and catch their prey as it passes by. They have big, shield-shaped heads which they use to close off the burrow when danger threatens. Their legs grip the tunnel walls, and special hooks on their backs anchor them firmly in their hidden homes. Root-feeding larvae have long, clinging legs and soft bodies. Their spiracles are covered with special filter plates that keep them from becoming clogged with soil particles. Some beetle larvae are fat, legless, eyeless grubs which merely stay in the same place when they feed. Such larvae are those living in enclosed places such as in wood or inside nuts or seeds.

Whenever an insect grows, it must shed its old cuticle and secrete a new, larger one. Most beetle larvae shed their old skins three times before becoming pupae, but a few do it many more times. Some have fourteen larval stages. Often, in kinds with many larval stages, the number varies depending on temperature, humidity, or food availability.

The Beetle Pupa

Once it is fully grown, the beetle larva stops eating. Leaf-eating larvae may drop from the plants and burrow into the soil, and predatory ones are likely to burrow, too. Sometimes they travel several feet underground, where

Some beetle larvae, like these grubs of a longhorn beetle in an oak tree, are very different from the more developed larvae of other species. These grubs and various other insects are used for food in some parts of the world.

moisture and temperature are more constant than above ground and where they will be protected from predators while they change into adult beetles. Wood-boring larvae generally bore close to the surface of the wood and so make the exit of the beetle easier.

At the end of its new burrow, the beetle larva hollows out a space in which the pupa can rest and then becomes inactive for a while. Finally the last larval skin is shed and the beetle becomes a pupa. During the process of shedding, the wings appear. They have been growing inside out within its body, and now they are turned right side out. Most of the other adult body features can also be seen on the outside of the pupa. The transformation from larva to adult in beetles is not as spectacular as it is in butterflies, since most beetle larvae already possess the adult structures, if in a simpler form. Hidden beetle pupae especially look like beetles. Their appendages are not stuck down to the surface of the pupa and can even move. The pupal cuticle has spines on it which hold the pupa off the floor of the burrow. Thus air can move freely around it and mold cannot grow.

A few beetles, such as ladybirds, have exposed pupae. The larva merely glues itself to a leaf and sheds its skin. The legs of such pupae are plastered down against the pupal body, protecting them from damage. One might think that such pupae would be easy prey to hungry animals, but they are often camouflaged—as bird droppings, for example. A few beetle larvae spin cocoons for themselves. For silk, they use the same material from which the membrane surrounding the mass of food in the intestine is made. The material is either spun out as a silk thread or made into leaf-shaped ribbons of chitin which are used to construct the cocoon.

The amount of time the beetle spends as a pupa depends on different factors. Some beetles rest through the winter or through the dry season buried safely as pupae, while others break out as soon as the adult beetle inside the pupal case is completely formed. After emerging from the pupa, the adult beetle usually waits in the burrow until its cuticle has hardened. It then uses its jaws to cut its way out and emerges into the outside world ready to live through the last and often shortest part of its life cycle.

Five

Water and Deserts for Homes

Both the water and the desert are difficult places for insects to live. In the water, oxygen is hard for insects to get, since they are basically adapted to live in air. In the desert, of course, it is the water that is hard to get. Beetles, like all other animals, need water for their bodies to function. But too much water combined with too little oxygen creates problems which different water beetles have "solved" in different ways. Desert beetles, on the other hand, must conserve what little water is available and also must have ways to deal with the extremely high desert temperatures.

Whirligig Beetles

Some water beetles spend most of their time on the surface where they can easily get oxygen from the air. Whirligig beetles swim on the water surface in circles when disturbed, often holding tightly in a group, whirling about in what looks like a frantic way. These shiny, streamlined insects are often not recognized as beetles, even when they are quite familiar. They belong to one family (the Gyrinidae) and most of them look very much alike. Whirligig beetles do much of their living on the top of the water, partly in air and only partly under the surface. Their bodies are supported by the surface tension. They feed upon small insects which drop or are blown into the water.

Life on the surface is especially dangerous, since fishes from below and birds from above might attack. Fortunately, with this double threat, whirligig beetles have remarkable eyes. Each eye is split in half so that the beetle really has four well developed eyes. Half of each of the original eyes is located on the bottom of the head and the beetle can look straight down into the water beneath. Since water is different from air, light waves going through each require a special eye form. The structure of the bottom eye is not the same as that of the other half, which has remained on top of the head and is adapted for vision in air.

Another thing one notices about a whirligig beetle is that the legs are very different from one another. In fact, these beetles at first seem to have only one pair, which sticks out toward the front. These obvious legs are used for grabbing the prey upon which the beetle feeds, and they look more or less like the legs of other beetles. The second and third pairs of legs are highly modified for swimming and too short to be seen fully from above. These very small legs are used for swimming and steering. The individual parts are wider than usual, turning them into paddles. These legs are fringed with flattened hairs, making the surface of the "paddle" larger and thus able to push harder against the water during swimming.

*One might think a whirligig beetle
is two-legged, at first view.*

A problem develops in using paddles located where the
legs of a beetle are usually found. When one paddles a
canoe, one can lift the paddle out of the water for the
return stroke. One doesn't undo the work just done in the
pushing stroke when one returns the paddle to the starting
position. The beetle, however, cannot remove its legs from
the water for this purpose. But whirligig beetles can tele-
scope the outer segments of the leg into the base piece
for the return stroke. This greatly reduces the leg surface
area and makes it possible to move the leg forward without pushing too hard against the forward movement of
the beetle.

This system works very well, since whirligigs are probably the fastest-swimming water beetles. When swimming on the surface, so that part of it is in the air, a whirligig beetle can move up to one meter, or about 200 of its body lengths, per second. When diving and totally under water it cannot move at more than one tenth of this speed, for water offers much more resistance than air. Whirligig beetles are very streamlined, which reduces the water resistance, and they are very maneuverable. The short swimming legs are also used to make course corrections, which can be done very rapidly. This combination of speed and agility makes it quite a challenge to catch these beetles with anything but a very wide-mouthed net. They can evade small vessels such as jars with no trouble at all.

Whirligig beetles may even be able to detect objects in front of them by a primitive form of "sonar" which uses waves on the surface of the water rather than sound waves to detect objects. They have a jerky swimming motion, and each stop and start sends a series of waves out all around the beetle like ripples from a pebble thrown into the water. When waves moving out in front of the beetle strike an object, they will reflect off it and go back toward the beetle. Whirligig beetles can probably detect such reflected waves and turn sharply to avoid the object ahead. No wonder they are so hard to catch!

Diving Beetles

Diving beetles (Dytiscidae) are smooth, sometimes quite large beetles which swim completely beneath the water rather than on the surface like the whirligigs. Their flattened bodies are well suited for minimizing drag as they swim through the water without sacrificing stability. The most streamlined shape for a water beetle would be that of a teardrop, but there is none with a shape of this kind. Such a beetle propelling itself through the water would find it almost impossible to stay on course. The slightest unevenness in the movement of the swimming legs, or a push from one side by a water current, would throw the beetle into a tailspin. The more disklike shape of diving beetles is still quite streamlined but a lot more stable.

Diving beetles get power from their legs for swimming and face some of the same problems the whirligig beetles do. But they have solved them somewhat differently. In most species, it is mainly the hind legs which provide the force for swimming. If you look at one, you will notice that the hind legs are covered with long golden hairs. In dead specimens, or in live ones out of the water, these hairs are plastered down against the leg. However, there is a joint at the base of each hair which permits it to be extended during the power stroke of the leg. The beetle spreads the hairs like a fan, providing almost all of the force which moves the insect forward. At the end of the power stroke, the hairs are pressed against the leg, thus streamlining it for the return stroke.

Diving beetles have modified the rhythm by which they move their legs, too, providing greater stability than is given by the usual pattern used by a walking insect. Both middle legs are moved at the same time, and then both hind legs together. This produces an equal push on each

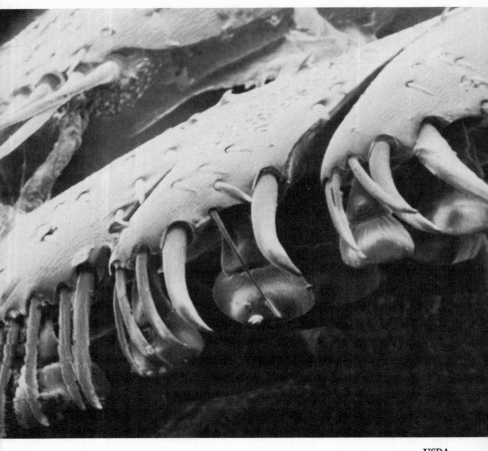

Side view of the tarsus (roughly equivalent to the human calf) on the first leg of a predacious diving beetle, highly magnified. The whole tarsus is widened into a disk, which helps the hind legs in swimming. The claws and suction cups are adaptations that help hold the rounded bodies of small fish that are among its prey.

side of the beetle at once, so that it does not tend to turn off course. The same pattern in a land beetle would probably make it fall flat on its face.

Since they spend so much time under water, diving beetles have to face the problem of getting oxygen when they are submerged. The larger beetles must come up for air every once in a while, and the air is stored in a bubble under the elytra.

Useful Bubbles

A number of water beetles, including the diving beetles, use an interesting "gimmick" which allows them to stay under water for fairly long periods. Like other insects, water beetles rely on their tracheal system to obtain and distribute oxygen. They must return to the surface to renew their supply of oxygen, like whales and seals in the sea. Beetles have perfected the trick of carrying bubbles with them beneath the surface of the water. But the oxygen present in such a bubble cannot last very long, and the bubble wouldn't be nearly as successful and useful to the beetle if only this oxygen were available.

But oxygen can dissolve in water, and dissolved oxygen is usually present in large quantities in fresh-water environments. Most aquatic organisms, including fish, use oxygen dissolved in the water for respiration. Bubble-bearing water beetles are no exception, even though they must have the oxygen in the form of a gas, and not dissolved in the water, before it will do them any good. As the beetle uses up the oxygen in the air which makes up its bubble, oxygen from the adjacent water tends to replace it. As long as the beetle can manage to keep the bubble there, it can get oxygen from it. This system is called "plastron respiration," and it is enough to provide all the oxygen needed by small beetles for hours at a time. "Plastron" in this use means a film of air lying against an aquatic insect.

Larger beetles cannot get enough oxygen this way and must surface periodically to fill their tracheae from the air and to get a new bubble. The plastron system works because of the nitrogen in air. Even if all the oxygen is removed from a bubble, it is still more than three-quarters of its former size because of the nitrogen, which is not used in respiration. If the bubble were made of pure oxygen, the whole thing would tend to get used up, leaving no gas behind for the oxygen from the water to move into. Plastron respiration is marvelously efficient and is based on the properties and behavior of the atmospheric gases. Some insects which rely heavily on a plastron have developed a dense mat of hairs in the location of the bubble which makes it more difficult to get the spot wet and protects the precious bubble from being pushed aside by seeping water.

Desert Beetles

Deserts of course are dry places. That is what the word means. In most people's minds, deserts are associated with extremely hot weather, which is true for most deserts for at least part of the year. But there are also northern deserts at fairly high elevations which can experience severe cold, and such deserts are inhabited by small numbers of plants and animals. The drier a place is, the fewer the kinds of plants which can grow. And the fewer types of plants there are, the fewer kinds of animals there can be. Deserts that receive a little water each year are usually much more interesting than those which receive almost none, because the plants and animals have at least a little to work with. Even a small reliable water supply can support an amazing diversity of plants and insects, especially beetles. Many of the beetles in deserts are slow, lumbering, black darkling beetles (Tenebrionidae).

A special type of environment occurs frequently in deserts, although it is not restricted to them. This is the sand dune, a place where few plants can grow because of the looseness of the sand, which tends to blow around easily. There is also a group of sand-loving beetles specialized for life in this specific and difficult environment. One particular desert, the Namib desert along the coast of southwestern Africa, is particularly interesting for the number of specialized beetles which live in it.

The sand dunes in the Namib desert are unusual in that no vegetation at all grows on them. They are part of a desert along several hundred miles of African coast where less than five inches (about 13 centimeters) of rain falls each year. In some years there is no rain at all. This desert appears to be an old and stable one, and it is very unusual in that a whole group of darkling beetle species has populated the barren dunes. At first sight it is not clear what could support any organism in this constantly shifting landscape.

But the winds bring two things which are very constant and upon which the beetles can rely: fog from the ocean, which brings some water; and debris from the highlands back from the coast, which accumulates in the troughs away from the wind behind the dunes. This very dry material, bits of dead plants and insects which lived elsewhere, appears to be the major source of food for these interesting animals, and the fog is their major source of water. Animals from one night-active genus dig trenches in the sand during a fog. The trenches have two built-up sides which extend just a little above the smooth surface of the dune. This little bit of added height intercepts some of the fog as it moves past, and the sand in the ridges becomes wetter than the flat sand next to them. The beetles then return along the ridge, flattening it and in some way extracting water from the wetter sand. Another species that lives on the dunes simply sticks its rear end up in the air and allows the fog to collect on its body. After a while, enough water will accumulate on the body surface to form drops which roll down to the legs, where the beetle can reach and drink them. There are probably other interesting methods by which such desert-dwellers take advantage of the moisture in the foggy air passing over them.

The dunes are high, wind-blown heaps of sand which offer protection from the merciless rays of the sun because of their height. The beetles probably could not live on a long stretch of flat sand. But as long as the dunes are present, they will cast shadows providing shade for relief from the hot desert sun. Furthermore, the dunes cause debris blown from further inland to drop from the air and accumulate on the side of the dune away from the wind. They thus concentrate the food supply.

Many other desert beetles are most active during the day after the fog has burned off. They are exposed to the full force of the sun. They take advantage of the fact that the sand is always blowing and being lifted up. This makes burrowing particularly easy, more like swimming through a fluid than digging through something solid. They can thus "dive" down into the sand to cool off and get away from the sun when they start to get too hot. The sand is much cooler a few inches down. Except close to noon, they can also usually find a shadowed spot on the dune. These beetles spend their lives at higher temperatures than most and they tend to be able to run faster than other darkling beetles. They spend the night buried in the sand.

The Black-Beetle Problem

For over fifty years scientists interested in the biology of deserts have been puzzled by the fact that a number of desert animals are black. This includes almost all of the desert darkling beetles we have been discussing. The fact that these beetles are black represents a problem because black things absorb more energy from the sun than light things and tend to warm up. Thus a black car may feel warm to the touch even on a cold, hazy day. It has absorbed energy efficiently from the small amount of sunlight getting through the haze. Since deserts are always thought of as hot places, it is usually assumed that animals which live there must constantly struggle to avoid being overheated and dehydrated, as human beings in the desert must. Yet a black darkling beetle was once observed near

Jerusalem walking across sun-warmed soil measuring
145° F (63° C). Others have been recorded as active on
surfaces which measured 135° F (57° C). The problem is,
how did these black beetles avoid absorbing so much
energy from the sizzling sun that they would suffer heat
prostration and subsequent death?

More recently, observations and experiments on some
of the Namib desert beetles have given us a basis for
understanding the problem. In the laboratory, it is possible to find out how hot a beetle can get before it dies,
and such measurements have been made on a number of
species. Beetles from this region can survive for 30 minutes at temperatures ranging from 113–124° F (45–51° C).
It is now possible to measure the temperature of the beetle
itself as it walks around. Amazingly enough, the beetles
like to be hot, and they arrange their lives to try and be
as hot as they can stand for as much of the day as possible.
The temperature they prefer is just a few degrees under
the temperature which could kill them.

In this respect they are like people and other mammals.
Normal human body temperature is expected to be about
98.6° F (37.1° C). An increase of body temperature to
about 107° F (about 41.5° C), an increase less than 10° F,
is extremely dangerous and can be fatal for adult humans.
We thus also keep our bodies very close to the temperature which might be fatal. We regulate our temperature
physiologically, especially by sweating. The beetles regulate their temperature behaviorally instead. When they
start to get too hot, they burrow into the sand, where it
is much cooler a few inches down. When they get too
cool, they expose themselves lengthwise to the sun, thus
getting maximum benefit from it.

The reason the beetles are black, at least in the Namib, appears to be that getting warm in the morning when the sun is rising and keeping warm in the evening, when the sun is setting, represent more of a problem than keeping cool in the heat of the midday sun. The black color helps

Black beetles, such as this darkling beetle, have a physio-logical problem in hot sun, for black objects absorb heat radiation more strongly than light-colored objects. However, when the sun is weak, as at the beginning and end of the day, they can keep sufficiently warm longer, so their color is also an advantage.   DR. JAMES E. LLOYD

them warm up and become active earlier in the morning than they otherwise could. In this way they can have a longer period of activity in the morning before things get so hot that they are forced to escape the midday heat beneath the sand. They emerge from the sand again in late afternoon for another period of activity. By being black, they can continue to absorb heat from the setting sun and keep their body temperature high longer. This extends their active period at the end of the day, too.

Beetles can do other things to keep their bodies at the temperature they prefer. They can move into a breeze or into the shadow of a rock or plant to cool off, and they can do the opposite to warm up. They can raise themselves high off the ground to permit cooling air to pass beneath them, or they can lie close to the ground to pick up heat from it. One particularly long-legged Namib darkling beetle is well-suited for this kind of activity. These beetles have been reported to stand on stones or pebbles to raise themselves out of the hottest layer of air (which is closest to the ground). On a flat plain, beetles will even fight to retain their higher and cooler perch when the desert heat becomes extreme.

The study of desert beetles has produced some surprising results. The beetles have helped us understand that even "cold-blooded" animals may prefer high body temperatures and that they can achieve them almost as well by doing the right thing at the right time as we can with our "warm-blooded" physiology.

Six

The Highly Successful Dung Beetles

To us humans, animal dung is not attractive material; in fact, we are repelled by it. But to many insects, dung is a rich source of food. Animals such as cows and sheep digest only a fraction of the useful food material in the plants they eat. Their dung also swarms with bacteria, which are a nutritious and easily digested food in themselves. Within a few minutes of being released by a cow, a dung pat is being explored by a variety of insects. Flies of many kinds lay their eggs there, and beetles whose larvae eat the fly maggots also deposit their eggs. Parasitic wasps are attracted and inject their eggs into hapless fly and beetle larvae. Competition for this unlikely-seeming but rich food source is intense.

Some highly successful scarab beetles have found ways of avoiding much of the competition and danger from predators which exists in and around the dung heap. These thousands of species of sturdy beetles range in size from less than one centimeter to more than five centimeters long. Some of the huge, heavily armored and powerful dung beetles live in Africa and Asia and are adapted to feed on the gigantic mounds of dung left by elephants. Dung beetles are built for burrowing, and while a few kinds may feed directly on the edge of a pile of dung, most cart it away before feeding. By hoarding their share of dung in burrows, these beetles avoid the prolonged competition and danger faced by insects which remain in the dung heap.

Many kinds of dung beetles burrow under the edge of the dung upon arrival. They tunnel beneath it, some forming complex burrows with many side branches. They then carve out chunks of dung, carry them into the burrows, and pack them into compartments for future feeding. Other species busy themselves carving out a portion of dung. Instead of burying their food near the source, these remarkable beetles form it into a ball and roll it off to a quiet spot, away from the bustling dung heap. There they bury it and then feed in utmost privacy. If many dung beetles arrive at the same cow pat, it may be reduced to nothing but a thin, hardened crust within 24 hours.

Dung-Beetle Adaptations

The variety of dung beetles is truly bewildering. Some will attack just about any kind of dung, while others are specialized for feeding on only one kind. Most dung beetles live in open pastures, where plant-eating animals are concentrated, but many inhabit open woodlands, utilizing the dung of mammals which live there. While some dung beetles fly only at night, others are active in the daytime. The specialized adaptations of these insects also extend to the temperature, soil type, moisture level, and season of the year.

The dung beetle's body is well-suited to its peculiar way of life. While the beetle's body is rather fat and rounded, the front edge of the head is thin, like the blade of a shovel. It has heavy, rakelike front legs which are used to shovel dung and for digging. The mouthparts of dung beetles are adapted for eating soft, pasty food. They are rich in fine hairs which can feel and screen very small particles, as small as bacteria. They can grind their food into minute bits, destroying eggs of potential parasites which have been laid in the dung. Vision is poorly developed in these creatures which spend most of their time underground. They search for their food on the wing and are attracted by its scent. While hunting for food, a dung beetle generally flies in a low, straight path over the fields. If it gets a whiff of dung, it flies closer to the ground in a zigzag path and may land several feet away and walk the rest of the way to its find.

In temperate regions, adult dung beetles emerge in the mid- to late summer. They feed on into the fall and pass the winter in deep burrows. The beetles may need to find several different sources of dung during their adult lives to nourish them before they are mature enough to reproduce. In hot places, like most of Africa, the dung-beetle life cycle depends on the annual rains. In very cold climates, such as central Asia, dung beetles may have a very long life cycle lasting two or even three years.

In most insects, the larval stage is longer than the adult one, but in dung beetles this tendency is reversed. The larval stage is short, while the adult feeding stage is usually quite long. The larvae are provided with just enough food for them to complete their development, so the adults must feed further to provide the energy for making eggs and sperms. Much variety exists in the nesting behavior of these insects. While some kinds merely prepare a burrow under the food and pack one end with dung on which an egg is laid, most kinds take more care in assuring the food supply and safety of the next generation.

The Brood Pear

Most dung beetles prepare a special package of dung for each egg laid. After digging a brood burrow, the female beetle carefully strains and sorts the dung for her offspring, kneading it and shaping it into a ball. She coats the ball with a clay shell and lays an egg on top. Then she shapes up the outer edges of the clay around the egg, enclosing it into a tiny, separate compartment on top of the dung. The final product—a protected package containing everything needed to produce a new dung beetle —is called a "brood pear" because of its shape. When the larva hatches out, it breaks through the thin clay layer separating the egg chamber from the food and begins to feed.

The dung-beetle larva is a strange-looking creature. It has strong jaws and no eyes. It is bent in the center and has a big hump in the middle of its back. If removed from the brood pear, it looks quite helpless and is unable to move about. But its peculiar shape adapts it well for life within its cramped home. While it feeds, the larva braces itself against the walls of the cavity produced by its feeding activities by wedging its hump and rear end. This leaves the small head free to move along the wall of the

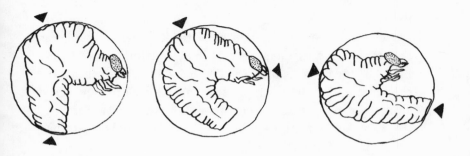

Left, a dung beetle larva in feeding position inside its dung ball; pointers show where the hump and rear end are wedged against the wall. At center, the larva has wedged its hump and head against the wall and swings its rear end forward to change position. Right, it is again wedged in by hump and rear end, now free to feed on a different part of the cavity wall. Drawing by co-author Patent.

cavity, scraping with its jaws. The larva moves its head up and down, rasping away at the food within reach. When it needs to move, it jams its head against the wall and releases its hind end. Now the head and the hump hold its body in place. The rear is shortened, swung forward, and pressed against a new part of the wall. The larva then releases its head, wedging itself in once again with the hump and the tail end. In this way it can move around quite nicely inside its small, dark cavity, always keeping it rounded, and always having it just the right diameter for wedging its body in place. What seems like an awkward and helpless creature is actually built just right for the life it leads.

While it lives and grows, the larva coats the walls of its home with its own excrement, which means that it also recycles the food more than once through its own digestive system. It extracts every bit of nutriment from the food left for it by its mother. The outer clay shell protects the larva and its food supply from attack by other hungry animals or by parasites and prevents both food and larva from drying out. If somehow a hole is punched in the brood pear, the larva can repair it by using its feces and secretions from its mouth. The brood pear is such a perfect, self-contained and protected place for the dung-beetle larva to develop that each female beetle need lay only a few eggs to ensure that some of her offspring live to maturity. Most insects must lay dozens or hundreds or even thousands of eggs, but dung beetles have developed such protected homes for their offspring that the single ovary of a female dung beetle produces only a minimal number of eggs during her lifetime.

Caring Parents

Ideal as the typical dung-beetle brood pear is for the larvae, some dung beetles go a step further in assuring the safety of their young. These beetles form long-lasting pairs and the females (sometimes also the males) remain with the developing young until they emerge as adult beetles. In one such species, the male finds the female in her feeding burrow before either is ready to mate. They feed there together, forming a partnership which lasts throughout the entire period of nest-building and food-storing.

As egg-laying time approaches, both the male and the

female collect dung to form a large cake within the burrow. The cake is then divided into four separate balls, and the female lays an egg in a hollow at the top of each ball. The male beetle leaves after the food has been collected and divided, but the female remains for the whole four-month period of larval development. She does not coat the brood balls with clay; she is there to assure that they serve their function. She wanders constantly over the balls, cleaning their surfaces of mold, patting them, and repairing any crumbling or cracking. She remains until the adult beetles emerge from the brood balls and accompanies her grownup offspring out of the burrow to the surface of the earth.

Close relatives of this beetle make from two to eight brood balls. One kind, which produces only two, builds its nest under pats of sheep dung. Both parents remain within the nest, but apparently only the female actually takes care of the brood.

The Sacred Scarab

Although beetles in general have not played an important part in the expression of human imagination, one beetle has. The sacred scarab of ancient Egypt belongs to the group of ball-rolling dung beetles. The sun-worshiping Egyptians saw the scarab as a mystical creature. They likened its rolling of a dung ball to the daily passage of the sun across the sky. They knew that the beetle buried its ball and that later more beetles would appear crawling out of the ground. The scarab became a symbol of rebirth after death, and the sun god Khepri was thought of as a giant scarab rolling the sun across the sky. Because of its connection with death and rebirth, the scarab was often used as a decoration in tomb art. In later centuries, a bit of stone carved into a scarab symbol was considered good luck, even into Roman times.

The sacred scarab and its relatives are especially fascinating creatures. These beetles avoid the competition for space around and under a dung heap by cutting off a piece of dung, shaping it into a ball, and rolling it away. They are adapted mostly for life in an open habitat, with few rocks and little leaf litter, although a few kinds do live in the forest.

The process of cutting and shaping the ball takes from ten to forty minutes. The beetle cuts a chunk out of the dung, using its head and forelegs. It pats and shapes this into a round ball. As it adds more and more dung, the ball is rolled about while being held by the sharp claws on the long hind legs. Now and then the beetle pats the ball with its front legs. A four-centimeter (1½-inch) beetle can build up and roll a ball the size of a small apple.

Experiments with ball-rollers have shown that the hind legs are used to measure the size of the ball, for if they are removed, the beetle cannot make it perfectly spherical any more. It has some way of sensing the weight of the ball as well. If a piece of lead is placed at its center, the ball is torn apart, the lead removed, and the ball reshaped. The beetles are also very versatile if presented with dung in different shapes. A flat disk is shaped into a ball by pulling up all the edges, while a narrow cylinder is simply rolled up. Small pellets are gathered and pressed into a ball, while a ball impaled on a pointer is cut in half, removed from the pointer, and stuck back together again.

After the ball is formed, the beetle mounts it with its hind legs and moves off, walking backward, head down, with the ball rolling along between the hind legs. While this is the method used by most dung beetle species, a few pull the ball along rather than push it. Some scarabs go only a short distance (perhaps 30 centimeters—essentially a foot) while others continue rolling for as far as 15 meters (16 yards). The beetle may roll for only two minutes or for a half hour. The burying place is carefully chosen, and the beetle may stop and inspect the ground several times before finding a satisfactory spot. Once it is satisfied, it makes a simple burrow and packs the dung into it. There it feeds continuously until the food is all gone. Then off it goes to search for more. The adult beetle may go through this process of searching, ball-forming, rolling, and eating 20 times before being ready to reproduce.

How Ball-Rollers Reproduce

The meeting of male and female scarab is a simple thing. They find one another at the food source, touch briefly, and become partners immediately. If two beetles are rolling a ball together, the chances are that they are a mated pair. Some dung beetle pairs cooperate in making and rolling a ball. One partner pushes while the other pulls. In some kinds, however, the work of ball-rolling is left to the male. The female follows a couple of centimeters behind or hitches a ride, balancing herself nimbly on top of the rolling ball like a dog in a circus.

The dung ball which the male and female roll is gen-

*A dung beetle, Canthon, manipulates its dung ball. Their un-
even ride on such balls has given dung beetles the common
name of "tumblebug."*

erally destined to be larval food. Because of the ways their bodies are modified for rolling balls, such as having longer, more slender legs, ball-rollers cannot dig as well as many other dung beetles. Therefore their nests are much simpler, although most ball-rollers do manage to bury their larval food balls. Some kinds coat the balls with clay, while others do not. The male of some kinds helps build the underground nest, but the female always shapes the brood pears. After the male leaves, the female tears apart the dung ball and puts it back together again, making a more compact structure. Perhaps this activity also helps to destroy any parasite eggs which might be present, for brood balls seem to be free of worm and insect eggs.

After spending 40 or 50 minutes reshaping the ball, the female climbs onto one side and pulls down bits of it. She moves all around the ball, doing the same thing, until an urn-shaped ball remains. She then climbs on top and smooths out a chamber on top for the egg. All this takes another hour or two. Finally, she lays her eggs and pulls up the rim of the depression over the egg, enclosing it in a small cavity on top of the dung, leaving only a small opening through which air can get in. She then pushes more dung up toward the top, turning the gourd-shaped structure into a pear-shaped one, coats it with soil from the floor of the nest, and finally leaves. The whole process, from shaping the brood ball to leaving the nest, may take as long as seven hours. The number of brood balls prepared in this fashion varies with the species. Some may make only three, while others prepare as many as ten in their lifetimes.

Fossil Dung Balls

Sometimes strange round fossils are found in large numbers buried in the ground, especially in South America. Some are hollow and some are solid. These are the fossilized remains of dung-beetle brood balls. The hollow ones contained larvae which never developed completely. The organic matter inside decayed away while the outer clay shell became fossilized. The solid ones represent successful balls which produced adult beetles. They show on their surface round exit openings through which the adult beetles emerged. Giant balls as big as 87 millimeters (almost three and a half inches) in diameter have been found. Their walls are 20 millimeters (slightly over three-quarters of an inch). Interestingly enough, the giant beetles which made these huge balls lived at the same time as many giant mammals. Just why the period was characterized by both giant mammals and giant beetles is not fully understood. Modern relatives of these over-sized extinct beetles produce balls 45 millimeters (about one and three-quarters of an inch) in diameter at the largest, with walls half as thick as the big fossil ones.

The Australian Problem

The native mammals of Australia are all marsupials such as the kangaroo and the wallaby. They produce rather small, dry dung pellets, high in fiber content. The 250 or so species of native Australian dung beetles are adapted to feed on these pellets and do not care for the larger,

moister pads of cow dung. When Europeans settled in
Australia, they brought their cattle with them. Since the
native beetles could not deal with cattle dung, it remained
on the ground for months or years, dried to hard cakes.
Eventually wind, weather, trampling, and feeding by
termites got rid of the dung. As long as there were few
cattle, their dung was not a problem. But as more and
more people raised larger and larger herds, difficulties
developed. A single cow drops an average of twelve pads
of dung each day. Five cows will cover the equivalent of
one acre of pasture in one year. The accumulated dung
becomes a breeding ground for biting flies and lessens the
grazing area of the pasture. Around the edges of the pad,
weeds grow which cattle will not eat unless they are
desperate. There are now over thirty million head of cattle
in Australia, a number which can cover six million acres
of pastureland with dung each year.

The Australian government has dealt with this problem
by the careful introduction of assorted dung beetle species
from Africa. The beetles had to be chosen carefully. Only
strictly pasture-dwelling kinds have been used. The climate in their native land had to correspond fairly well
with that of their new homes, and a careful mixture of
day and night species, buriers and rollers, had to be used.

The Australian government made its decision in 1963 to
introduce the dung beetles. Because of the possible problems which introduced species might cause, it was 1967
before the first beetles were actually released. Scientists
had to be certain that the insects would not bring with
them any serious cattle diseases found in Africa. In exam-
ining adult dung beetles, they found that they carry many

kinds of mites which could conceivably carry diseases. Nematode worms, which are often parasites, were found lodged under the elytra, and various kinds of fungi and bacteria thrived in the beetle cuticle and intestine. The beetles thus seemed like walking zoos, potentially introducing all sorts of other living things along with themselves.

In order to eliminate all these fellow travelers, scientists in South Africa began a painstaking process of artificial dung beetle culture. They removed the eggs from brood balls of African species. The eggs were washed in a detergent solution, immersed for three minutes in a formalin solution, drained, and carefully rinsed in sterilized distilled water. They were then packaged in damp, sterilized peat moss sent in sealed containers to Australia. There the eggs were transferred into artificial balls made with Australian dung. The balls were buried carefully in moist, sandy soil. Then all the scientists could do was to wait hopefully until weeks later when adult beetles emerged from the soil. These were allowed to mate and make their own balls. The eggs were again removed from the natural balls, sterilized, and transplanted. Only now were they considered safe for exposure in Australia, and mass rearing of the "purified" beetles was begun.

By 1970, 275,000 beetles of four species had been released, mainly in the northern, tropical parts of Australia. One kind, the gazelle dung beetle, was an immediate success and has spread all along the coast. These beetles can deal with the cow dung almost completely for part of the year, but other kinds are necessary to handle the problem the year around.

Controlling Pests

One serious problem associated with cow dung which remains on the ground is biting flies. Cow pads provide them with generous breeding grounds, and they have become serious pests throughout much of Australia. The native bush fly can make outdoor life unbearable for humans and animals alike in the Australian summer. Now that the gazelle beetle is abundant, these flies are less of a problem. If gazelle beetles attack dung containing bush fly eggs, they destroy almost all the fly eggs and maggots. The few maggots which escape have little food to eat and grow into stunted flies which cannot reproduce very successfully. But the gazelle dung beetle cannot control the buffalo fly, an introduced species which has a nasty habit of biting and feeding on blood. Buffalo flies are active in the early spring before the weather is warm and wet enough for this particular dung beetle. And the buffalo flies are still active for several weeks in the fall after the beetles are finished for the season.

Another problem associated with the introduced species of dung beetles is the marine toad. This oversized insecteater was introduced into Australia to control beetles which damage sugar cane roots. Unfortunately, not enough careful study was put into this introduction, for the marine toad shows little taste for sugar cane beetles. It prefers interesting and harmless native species. Since the introduction of dung beetles, the toads have developed the habit of hopping to fresh dung heaps and waiting to capture gazelle dung beetles as they arrive. One of these toads can consume as many as 80 beetles in one night, making a considerable dent in the dung-beetle population.

To outwit the toads, Australians are introducing large, powerful dung beetles. These enormous insects are the size of golf balls. One pair can bury a cow pat overnight, turning it into brood pears as big as baseballs. The beetles are active at dusk and dawn, just like the toads. But they are so large and strong that the toads pose no threat to them. Even if a toad was able to swallow one, the beetle could probably rip its way out of the toad's stomach, destroying the foolish predator in the process.

Helpful Insects

The problems in Australia have stimulated many studies which show just how important dung beetles are to the balance of nature. They eliminate a breeding ground for parasitic worms of cattle as well as for annoying flies. Cow pads which have been attacked by dung beetles produce fewer than half the number of parasitic worm larvae that untouched ones do. Some pads which the beetles have worked over produce almost no worms at all. Dung beetles also increase the fertility of the soil in several ways. They remove the concentration of unprocessed dung which can smother seeds and plants and distribute the fertilizer more evenly when they bury their food balls. Their burying activities also loosen up the soil, allowing water and air to get in. While they may seem to us to live rather unappealing lives, dung beetles play a vital part in nature's recycling of substances in the natural world.

Seven

Let There Be Light . . .

The flashing of fireflies has amazed and delighted people for generations, but only during this century have scientists taken to studying these fascinating insects seriously. They are quite common over much of the eastern part of the United States and most Americans are probably lucky enough to have seen the magical display of flashing, flying lights of fireflies at dusk. The name "firefly" has a certain poetry to it, but it is completely inappropriate. As was mentioned earlier, fireflies are not flies at all but small beetles. And the light they produce can in no way be compared to fire. Not only is the light under the complete control of the beetle, which can turn it off and on at will, but it is also completely cold.

It is easy to get confused when discussing fireflies. There are similarities among the more than 2000 species, but there are important differences as well. Fireflies generally live in damp places such as along streams and marshes or in meadows by the woods. The larvae are hungry carnivores which attack the snails and slugs that are also common in the same sorts of habitats. Firefly larvae have sharp, strong mandibles. The mandibles of at least one kind are hollow. When this larva finds a slug or snail, it grabs it with its strong jaws and injects a paralyzing poison. Enzymes are injected along with the poison and turn the tissues of the snail into a mush which the larva can suck back in through the mandibles and swallow.

While firefly larvae may live for as long as two years, the adult beetles survive only a few days or weeks. They are quite small (usually under half an inch) and inconspicuous when they are not emitting light. Their soft, flattened bodies are usually mostly black or brown, and they hide during the day. They have thin antennae and big eyes. The adults of some fireflies do not feed at all, while others are hungry predators.

What Is a Glowworm?

One easy source of confusion about fireflies is the existence of glowworms. This word is used for more than one thing. Some firefly larvae emit light; they are called glowworms. In addition, some kinds of fireflies have wingless females that resemble larvae and that emit light to attract the males; these are also called glowworms. While most fireflies and glowworms belong to the family Lampyridae, a few glowworms belong to the different but closely related family Phengodidae. Little is known about most members of this small family. They are generally rare and hard to find. One, called the railroad worm, has two bright red lights on its head and eleven pairs of yellowish green ones along the length of its body. Another kind, the European glowworm, has four lights on the underside of her abdomen. She glows continuously and attracts the

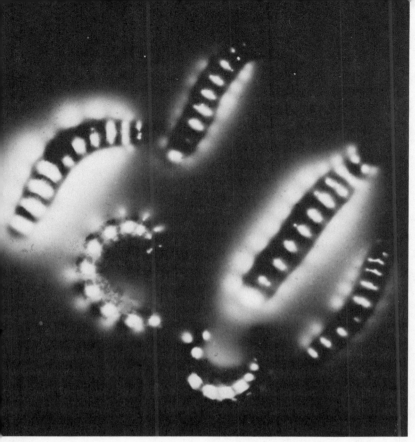

Glowworms, the wingless female larvae of certain fireflies, photographed by their own light.

nonglowing male with her light. Larva-like female Lampyridae, however, can turn their lights off and on.

No one yet understands why there are larval glowworms. While the existence of a glowing adult female which can attract the male makes sense, why should the larva, which it seems should be as inconspicuous as possible in order to avoid predators, advertise itself by glowing? Glowing itself does not seem to deter predators, for live toads with fat, glowing bellies full of fireflies or glow-worms have been seen by startled observers. Some fireflies even have glowing eggs, another mystery. Up to now, the scientists who have studied fireflies and glowworms have concentrated their attention on the short but spectacular period of the life cycle during which the insects are using their special light-producing equipment to attract one another. Perhaps eventually someone will devote study to the longer and less obvious early part of firefly life and be able to provide some ideas about the functions (if any) of light during that time.

Many Kinds of Lanterns

The light organs of fireflies are located on the underside of the rear abdominal segments. Some kinds have just one rather small lantern, while others have a pattern of several separate light organs. A common pattern consists of two large organs covering all or most of two segments. The typical firefly lantern consists of three different cell regions. The innermost region has cells which contain peculiar crystals. These may help reflect the light produced in the middle-region cells. These light-producing cells have microscopic tracheae right next to them which bring oxygen necessary for the light reaction. Inside the light-producing cells are many granules. They contain a special enzyme, called luciferase, which acts upon another chemical in the granules, luciferin, combining it with oxygen to produce light. The outermost layer of the light organ is soft, almost transparent skin through which the firefly glow is easily seen.

Glowworms and fireflies are not the only glowing beetles. Some click beetles that are called firebeetles have two kinds of light organs. Many species have a pair of lanterns on the pronotum and a single one on the underside of the abdomen. Although there is some evidence that firebeetles communicate with their lights, very little is actually known about them.

Mutual Attraction

The simplest sort of light communication is that found in some phengodids, in which the female simply glows all the time and the male comes to her. All lampyrids have one advantage over their less advanced relatives; they can turn their lights off and on. The European glowworm has inspired legend and song over the centuries. At dusk the larva-like type of glowworm female climbs up onto a blade of grass or other site from which she can be seen. She twists her abdomen so that the light organs on the underside are easily visible from above. She emits a continuous glow until she is spotted by a passing male. The males search for their shining mates by flying slowly, close to the ground. They can produce a little light themselves, but it is faint and seems to play no important role in courtship. When a male spots a female, he folds his wings and lands close to her. He is attracted to the color, size, and pattern of her light and is not very easy to fool. Experiments in the laboratory show that if the pattern and size are right, the color can vary somewhat from the natural yellow-green and still attract him.

Common American fireflies use quite a different system

to bring males and females together. The females of most have wings, but they rarely use them. They crawl up blades of grass at dusk and sit there, awaiting the males. The males fly about, flashing their bright lanterns. Each species of firefly has a particular signal used by the male. The simplest sort is a single flash of a certain length, followed after a second or two by another flash, and so forth. The female responds only to the flashes of a male of her own species. She answers him, after a pause of a certain length, with a single flash. He recognizes her answer by the length of time between his flash and hers. When a male sees a female flash correctly, he turns toward her and flashes again. If she answers, he continues to move toward her and flash. After a series of five to ten flash exchanges, the male is close enough to land and walk over to his new mate.

Some fireflies have a more complex system. The male signal consists of two or more flashes instead of one, and the female will respond only to that signal. Her response may also be more complicated. Because the "code" of each firefly species is different, several kinds can live and court in the same area without confusion.

Scientists take advantage of the firefly codes to capture them for study. By observing carefully, it is easy to figure out the male and female flash patterns of the different species. These can be imitated by using a penlight, and the fireflies are fooled. By reproducing the answering pattern of the female, male fireflies can be lured to land right on a hand-held penlight, and the hidden perches in the grass of the females can be discovered by imitating the male flash and watching for correct responses.

An Efficient System

The typical firefly method of attracting a mate is an extremely efficient one. The flying, flashing males are hard to track and the short flashes of the females are also tricky to locate. Since the active, flashing period may last

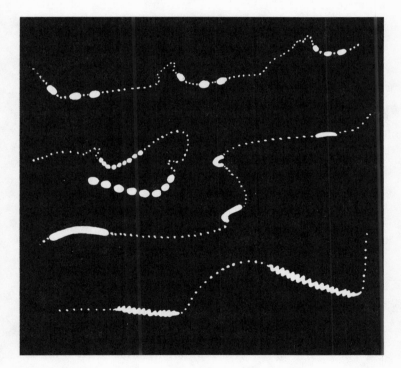

Firefly flash patterns of various species are seen here, as they would look in a time-lapse photograph. Dotted lines between flashes represent flight paths. Based on research by Dr. James E. Lloyd.

less than a half hour each evening (perhaps only a half hour of total time in the life of one female firefly), these insects are exposed to predators for a very short period of time. They use a minimum of time and energy in finding mates.

One flaw in this means of communication is that the flashing insects must be within the line of sight of each other in order to be seen. The twisting flight of the males is probably one way of getting around this; they expose their signals to many possible perches by varying their flight. The females can turn their abdomens and "aim" their flashes in the direction of the male's flash, and the female's signal follows closely enough after his that he has not moved too far since he flashed. The males also have very big eyes and so can see a large area around them.

It seems possible that starlight or moonlight might confuse fireflies. Perhaps this explains why some kinds are not very active during the full moon. Most fireflies have an enlarged pronotum which extends over the head and eyes; perhaps this helps screen out light from above such as starlight, which might otherwise interfere with their signal exchanges.

Communication using light is possible only at times or in places where natural light is dim or absent—in caves, under logs, in the deep sea, or at night. But it tends to be cold at night, and beetles cannot fly unless their bodies are warm enough. This is probably why North American fireflies are active usually right around dusk. None have their greatest activity period after midnight. In the tropics, where it is much warmer at night, many fireflies are active very late at night.

Firefly Trees

Some tropical fireflies have a most impressive way of advertising themselves. The males gather by the thousands in particular trees and flash in unison. Their synchrony is so close that between flashes the tree is almost completely blackened. One second the tree is lit up like a gigantic Christmas tree and the next it is dark. Natives and travelers alike have been awed and amazed by these displays for decades, but scientists have been able to study them only in the last ten years, since the areas where such fireflies live are often remote and hard to reach. But despite much hard work and a great deal of thinking, a clear understanding of how and why these beetles behave as they do has not yet been reached.

Traits such as firefly flashing are inherited; this means that they are passed from parents to offspring through the generations, just as hair and skin color are in humans. In each generation, the traits found will depend on which animals in the previous generation were successful in mating and leaving offspring. Thus we can say that the individual males of the synchronously flashing fireflies gain some mating advantage by flashing together, or this behavior would have disappeared by now. But it would seem that flashing in unison with other males is as likely to help the other males as to help the individual male himself. What advantage can he possibly have over the other males by cooperating with them? And from their point of view, what advantage can they have from co-operation with him? These are difficult questions to an-swer, but there are some clues.

Our native American fireflies live in open, grassy areas where they can easily see one another. But the tropical species which gather in the firefly trees live in tangled jungles, where the view is blocked by trees, bushes, and vines. Perhaps the firefly trees act as beacons, attracting fireflies from a wide area. It is true that both male and female fireflies are drawn to trees where members of their species are flashing. An individual male flying through the underbrush and flashing would have slight chance of be-ing seen by a female, but a male flashing on the leaf of a tree in unison with thousands of others of his kind would at least have a chance of meeting one of the attracted females. So perhaps being part of the huge display does not in itself give the male an advantage over other males in the display; it simply gives him his only chance of en-countering a female. Once she has landed on the tree, he must compete in some way or ways with the other nearby males for her attention.

But then another problem arises. What about males which have not bothered to join the display and flash? Why couldn't they merely land on the tree and "steal" the females with their individual lights? If this happened, and such males produced large numbers of offspring, the whole system would fall apart. The males which flashed together would be at a disadvantage and would leave fewer off-spring than the "cheaters," and in a few generations the "cheaters" would outnumber those which flash together.

The group flashing behavior would then gradually disappear. We know that this does not happen. Firefly species with group flashing have been around for a long time, and certain trees are "traditional" sites for the displays. One scientist observed the flash displays in the same tree for five straight years, and boatmen along rivers often use the trees as landmarks for navigation.

Since the synchronous flashing behavior keeps on generation after generation, group flashers must have an advantage over "cheaters." The simplest explanation for this success is that perhaps the females will respond only to males which flash in unison with their fellows. They might ignore the "cheaters" entirely. Then the individual males which do flash together could compete for the nearby females in other ways. Perhaps some have brighter lanterns than others and the females prefer to mate with these. Or perhaps other kinds of behavior are involved in the final stages of courtship. Close observation of fireflies in the tree shows that in addition to the bright chorused flashes, the males have dimmer, different flash patterns. Maybe these play a role in courtship. The actual behavior between males and females during the crucial last few moments before mating have not been observed and described, partly because neither insect flashes at this time. Thus it is possible that, despite the brilliance of the light display and its importance in bringing the sexes together, the final choice of a mate is made by the female based on cues which have nothing to do with the ability to shine.

A *female firefly*, Photuris versicolor, *waiting to mimic the flash responses of females belonging to other species. When a male responds to what would seem to be a mating invitation, it is eaten.*

Firefly Femmes Fatales

The French phrase *femme fatale* means "deadly woman," and is often used to describe a woman with the power to make men fall in love with her. The firefly *femmes fatales* live up to their nickname in a more literal fashion, for they actually lure males to their death, eating them once they have been captured. The females of 12 or more firefly species prey on males of other kinds. Females of at least one of these species can lure a male by mimicking the flash responses of females of his kind. These voracious "ladies" perch on grass blades awaiting potential victims. When a male of a prey species flies by, the predatory female responds as if she were a potential mate. If the male answers back, she repeats her flash and finally he is lured into her grasp.

The most amazing thing about these mimicking females is that they can "copy" the correct responses of more than one other species. The same predatory firefly may respond correctly to the flash patterns of at least four different prey species. Her responses are not always exact copies of the correct one; her timing (which is usually the most critical part of the female signal) is usually quite exact, while the actual pattern of her response may be less than perfect. She may be more effective in capturing some species than others, too. Just how the small firefly brain could develop such a sophisticated ability as to recognize the different male patterns and provide the proper response after the proper interval remains one of the mysteries of firefly biology.

Actually, we know very little of what there is to learn about fireflies. The majority of species have never been studied, and a substantial number of species still remain unnamed and unstudied, as researchers know by observing many unfamiliar flash patterns during their work. Nothing is known about the behavior of most of these fascinating insects, and surely many new and exciting discoveries await those who set out to fill in the huge gaps in our knowledge.

Eight

Interacting with Other Animals

Beetles do not live in a world by themselves. They are
influenced by the other animals which might eat them or
which they might eat or interact with in other ways.

Many animals, especially birds, eat beetles. But beetles
have evolved a number of interesting ways of protecting
themselves. The simplest way to avoid being eaten is to
get out of the way when danger is near. Beetles can either
fly away or just pull in all their legs and fall from their
perch. A surprisingly large number of beetles will drop
rather than fly. The beetle collector soon gets used to this
behavior and by placing a jar beneath a beetle on a branch
can capture it simply by moving the branch enough to
startle the beetle into dropping.

If it is not caught in a jar, such a fall will usually bring
the beetle into a tangled collection of sticks, stems, and
old leaves where it will be very difficult to find. A beetle
which has pulled in its legs will often remain in this pellet-
like pose for several minutes before venturing to extend
a leg or attempting to right itself. Such beetles are often
said to be "playing dead." Many of the animals which feed
upon beetles rely upon vision for detecting their prey, and

the easiest thing to see is movement. There is thus a real reason for remaining still for a while after dropping away from the stem or branch. Some kinds of beetles which drop never make it to the ground but spread their wings on the way down and start flying before they hit the ground. The flight of such individuals is especially difficult to follow, because one cannot be sure where it is going to start.

Some beetles have special avoidance mechanisms. For instance, the extremely fat hind legs of the very small flea beetles (Chrysomelidae) permit them to spring powerfully from their position on a leaf or stem in any direction if they are threatened. They are difficult to catch because of this habit. They ultimately fall to the ground like the beetles which simply drop, but it is more difficult to anticipate their direction.

The click beetles can jump without using their legs. These insects often simply fall from the vegetation when threatened. But they can continue to jump once they reach the ground if they happen to land on their backs. They are easy to recognize because of their long, slim bodies. Each beetle has a little peg on the underside projecting from between the front pair of legs to a point between the middle pair of legs. The peg is a part of the "click" mechanism used for jumping. The click beetle arches its back and wedges the peg against a special projection from between the middle legs.

Then it pushes very hard with certain muscles in the prothorax, above the front legs. This push gradually forces the peg from its position; after a moment it slips very suddenly. The front part (head and prothorax) snaps upward and the beetle soars into the air to a height of a foot or more, without opening its wings. This is primarily an escape mechanism, although very often the beetle which was on its back lands on its feet. Thus the trick also gets them out of a helpless position.

Flight may seem the most logical escape for an endangered beetle. But flying away is not as effective as it may at first seem. If a warmup period is required before the beetle can fly, it might not be able to get into the air in time. And of course, if it is threatened by a bird, there is no protection in the air. Thus there are several reasons why this most obvious escape response is often not the best.

Chemical Warfare

Many beetles use various forms of chemical warfare which have been only recently discovered by scientists. One form of chemical attack is releasing unpleasant-smelling chemicals which irritate a predator and make the beetle taste bad. Many ground beetles can squirt a very strong solution of formic acid from glands at the rear end when they are disturbed. This chemical irritates the skin and apparently tastes bad to predators. Collecting such beetles can leave brown stains on the hands where they have been attacked by small quantities of this corrosive solution. Some ground beetles can even spray strong formic acid behind them for a distance of ten times their own length.

One particular group of ground beetles has developed chemical defense to such an amazing degree that it is

recognized in their common name, the bombardier beetles. If one's hand closes over the hind end of one of these
fairly attractive-looking insects, when one picks it up
there will be felt a little hot spot on the fingers. At the
same time there will be a distinct but soft pop. This sound
is actually a small explosion just outside the rear end of
the irritated beetle. It carries a bit of a very concentrated
hydrogen peroxide solution inside a gland at the tail end.

Hydrogen peroxide is a highly reactive chemical, sometimes used in much more dilute solutions for bleaching
hair. It is dangerous because it is unstable. Bombardier
beetles have an enzyme which speeds up the natural
breakdown of the hydrogen peroxide into water and gaseous oxygen. The reaction gives off a lot of heat. The
oxygen reaches the temperature of boiling water, and at
this high temperature it requires much more room than is
available within the beetle's glands. The gas rushes out
so abruptly and violently that it makes the soft explosion
mentioned above. It is remarkable that the insect can
keep these dangerous chemicals within its body and cause
them to react only when it is alarmed. The explosion also
spreads around other bad-smelling, irritating chemicals.
The beetle can aim the spray so that it hits the offending
predator even if it is attacking from the front. The tip
of the beetle's abdomen can be curled down beneath the
body and aimed at an offending insect in front or to either
side. The tip of the abdomen can be rotated something
like an artillary turret.

The diving beetles are related to the ground beetles,
and may have evolved from them a long time ago. These
beetles also have glands at their posterior ends which

produce unpleasant chemicals, but in this case they serve a different function. After a diving beetle has been in the water for some days, a slimy growth of bacteria tends to grow on it, covering the whole outside surface. The chemical produced by the beetle is periodically smeared over its surface, serving as an antibiotic. It kills the bacteria and gets rid of the slime. If the slime were allowed to grow unchecked, it would ruin the smooth outline of the beetle and make its swimming much less efficient. The chemical is similar to those produced by ground beetles.

The diving beetles also produce another extremely interesting chemical which they use in their own defense. The main predators of diving beetles are not birds, but fish and amphibians. A pair of glands opening on each side just behind the head produce a milky secretion which has long been known to stun fish. Recently it was discovered that this secretion is produced also by fish; it acts as a hormone for the fish but not for the beetle. Hormones are chemicals which produce normal control of the activities of various parts of animal bodies, and they are required in very small amounts. When a fish or a frog eats a beetle producing large quantities of this particular hormone, the predator may throw up violently or even become paralyzed. The beetle even stands a reasonable chance of surviving after it has been swallowed. This is a very sophisticated form of chemical warfare. The beetles have been found to produce such large quantities of the hormone, compared with a fish, that for the chemist who wishes to study the hormone the beetles are a much better source of material.

Many darkling beetles also can release unpleasant com-

pounds from glands at the rear end of the body. In
so, the beetle perches on its six legs and looks as if
standing on its head; its rear end goes up in the air, w
ing the chemicals toward the threatening foe. Other species of darkling beetles which live in the same deserts as
the spraying beetles also "stand on their heads" when
threatened. But they cannot emit an unpleasant secretion.
They rely on the fact that predators have probably ex-
perienced the kind with unpleasant flavor and have come
to associate the tail-up posture with the unpleasant chemicals. An animal which resembles the unpleasant beetles
and assumes the same posture can secure almost as much
protection as if it actually had the secretions itself. But
some animals are undaunted by the beetle's threat. There
is a well known photograph of a grasshopper mouse eating one of the spraying beetles from the front while holding the rear end in the sandy desert soil to absorb the
unpleasant spray. Rarely is a defense mechanism perfect.

Small rove beetles of the genus Stenus use chemicals
secreted from glands in their rear ends for defense in
another interesting way. The many species of Stenus prefer to live near water. One kind uses glands at the rear
to provide it with a really fast escape should it fall or be
blown onto the water's surface. When such a small animal lands on water, it is too light to break through the
surface film but is held up by surface tension. Stenus,
standing on the water and threatened by a rapidly swimming whirligig beetle, releases a chemical from its rear
end which changes the surface tension properties of the
water just behind it. The beetle is jet-propelled over the
surface until its bumps into something solid and can es-

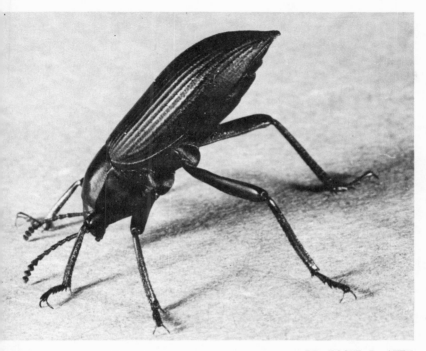

DR. ROGER D. AKRE

Eleodes, one of various bombardier beetles, runs about with its rear end up when disturbed and, if necessary, expels at a predator a chemical that explodes with a soft pop. It is one of the darkling beetles.

cape from the water. The chemicals the beetle uses for this have been identified. When they are mixed and carefully deposited behind a small piece of paper placed on the water, it zips across the surface just as the live beetle does. (One can experimentally get the same effect by putting a small blob of Plastic Wood on the edge of a bit of paper and dropping it on water.)

Poisonous Blood

Some beetles do not have special glands for their deterrent and distasteful chemicals; they simply store them within their bodies. Most species of blister beetles contain a potent poison in their blood called cantharidin. The beetles are called blister beetles because when grasped they start to bleed, usually at the joints of the legs. This exposes the predator to the poison-containing blood which can raise blisters on the skin. Cantharidin is also very effective in warding off attacks by predatory insects such as ants. The beetles seem to have complete control over which joint will start to bleed. If only one leg is grasped, only the joint of that leg will bleed. Stronger stimulation will cause bleeding in all the legs of the threatened side, but none from the other side. The threat must be very great to cause release of blood from the joints of all six legs. The chemical is probably most useful to the blister beetles in defense against other attacking insects. But despite their being so toxic, a few other insects do eat them. Such predators have apparently mastered the metabolic trick which keeps cantharidin from harming them, just as the blister beetles themselves have.

Ladybird beetles also can release blood containing unpleasant chemicals from their leg joints when they are threatened. It is thought that ladybirds' being often mostly orange or red makes them obvious and easily remembered by potential predators. The bright color may be a warning coloration, which is just the opposite from the camouflage used by beetles lacking chemical defenses. Its function is to advertise the beetle to potential enemies, making it easy to recognize and remember. Beetles which defend themselves chemically in this way have a tendency to occur in large, very obvious groups. Ladybird beetles aggregate into huge swarms during periods of cold or low food supply. They pile atop one another by the thousands, coating all available surface, be it rock, log, or ground, for an area of several square feet. Such aggregations would make them very vulnerable to predators if they were palatable, but just one report exists of grizzly bears possibly having eaten them. They are safe because of their "bad blood."

Hiding from Danger

If a beetle has no poisons, hormones, or explosives which can protect it, it can hide from its enemies either by matching its background and so avoiding being seen, or by simply hiding during the day. Many plant-eating beetles match their background. There are green weevils and shiny black metallic wood borers which crawl over fire-blackened wood in search of places to lay their eggs. Some weevils in New Guinea have gone to an extreme in camouflaging themselves. They live fairly high on the mountains there where the mountains are very frequently blanketed in cool fog, the so-called "cloud forest." Here the trees and rocks are all covered with small mosses, fungi, and lichens. The weevils, which are fairly large, quite slow-moving and flightless, have special places on their elytra in which fungi, lichens, and mosses grow. They seem to provide a sticky secretion that help the plants attach. In this way, their backs are covered with the same plants which cover the rest of their world. They not only look like the background, they carry the real thing around with them. It is also interesting that there are small animals which live in the small fungal and lichen forests on the backs of the weevils, including one type of mite which has been found nowhere else.

Many beetles are active almost exclusively at night, even though the temperature is usually lower then. Predation from animals (particularly birds) which have to see them before they can catch them, is much less at this time. Nocturnal beetles tend to be brown, black, or drab combinations of the two, and they tend to have eyes with fewer and larger facets than related day-active forms do. Many beetles tend to fly at night, and a large percentage are attracted by lights and will fly to them. Although the reason for this is not well understood, the fact permits the collection of night-active beetles which might otherwise be hard to find. There are many species of night-active beetles whose normal habits are almost totally unknown; they have been collected only at lights.

Taking Advantage of Ants

In addition to trying to protect themselves from animals which wish to take advantage of them, some beetles are specialized for taking advantage of other animals instead. This usually involves eating them. But there are also beetles which can make other insects feed them. This involves interesting relationships with social insects, particularly ants which live in complex colonies and build well structured nests.

In Europe, a beetle belonging to a family known as the sap beetles (Nitidulidae) intercepts worker ants on their way back to their nest after gathering food. Worker ants usually feed the ant larvae and other ants back in the nest with liquid material they bring back. They are signalled to do this when the ant wanting to be fed touches the mouthparts of the food-carrying ant in a special way. The beetle has somehow learned to do the same thing. Since ants are very mechanical creatures which respond primarily to standard odors in the colony and standard touching signals such as this, when the beetle touches the ant in the right way it will stop and feed the beetle. Not every ant is fooled, however. Some sense a difference and attack the beetle. When this happens, the beetle is prepared; it simply pulls in its legs and antennae and plays dead until the attack stops.

Other beetles, such as one particular kind of scarab, may live inside the ant nest itself. They actually eat the tender larvae which are being cared for in the nest by the worker ants. They too are well armored and can withstand the attacks of defending workers protecting the larvae in their charge. The beetles are frequently attacked when they are on top of the anthills, but seem to be safer once they have reached the inside of the nest. The beetle lays its eggs within the anthill and its larvae develop there. Both larvae and adults defend themselves from attacking ants with a secretion from glands at the rear end which smells bad. Larvae can also lash out and bite attacking ants, frequently giving them fatal wounds. These beetles do take advantage of the ants, but their lives are ones of constant harassment and defense.

Other kinds of beetles have integrated themselves more

nearly completely into the lives of the host ant colony and live in peace with them. They win over the ants by feeding them from glands which produce what must be delicious or even intoxicating secretions. The secretions are released onto characteristic tufts of golden hair called trichomes which the ants can lick. A small member of the family called the short-winged mold beetles (Pselaphidae) lives at peace within the colony of its host ant. There are trichomes on several portions of the body of this blind and flightless beetle which appear to be used most frequently by the younger larvae of the ants. They hang onto the hairs with their mandibles while the beetle walks around, dragging the larvae with it.

When the ant larvae are fed by workers, the larvae frequently regurgitate some apparently nutritious material which the workers pass along or consume. Feeding of the larvae by the workers is thus a process of exchange. The adult beetles frequently get the ant larvae to feed them as if they were exchanging food. The beetles, however return no food. Presumably they receive much more food this way than they give to the ants by way of the trichome secretions.

One remarkable little rove beetle has become involved in the life cycles of two different kinds of ants. This beetle (*Atemeles pubicollis*) takes advantage of the ants' chemical communication. Atemeles hatches in the nest of its first host (Formica) in the fall. It gets the ants to feed it by mimicking the touch signals which induce feeding. After a week or so it leaves that nest in search of the nest of a different ant (Myrmica). The beetle finds the nest by its odor, since the nests are hidden underground. Once at the new nest, the beetle lands and wanders around until it finds a Myrmica worker. The beetle offers it a secretion from a gland at its rear end which acts like the glands associated with trichomes; this organ is called an "appeasement gland." Then the ant licks another secretion from the "adoption glands" on the side of the beetle's body. This secretion somehow makes the ant pick up the beetle and carry it into the nest. The beetle folds all its legs and antennae in and allows itself to be carried.

Once in the new nest, the beetle settles down for the winter. The ants feed it and care for it until spring, when the beetle leaves in search of a Formica nest. Now the beetle responds only to the scent of Formica, not to that of Myrmica. It lays its eggs in the Formica nursery. There the beetle larvae hatch and grow. They beg food from worker ants and eat ant larvae. They become pupae and emerge as adult beetles to start the cycle all over again.

Beetle Parasites

Blister beetles also take advantage of social insects, this time various kinds of bees. Adult blister beetles lay their eggs on flowers, where they hatch into very small but very active larvae which wait for bees to visit the flower. When one arrives, the larva attaches itself and is carried to the bee's nest. Once there, the beetle larva attacks the bee eggs and larvae and molts into a different type of larva which cannot move fast at all. Now that it is in the presence of food, it need merely grow and eat. Some blister beetles attack the eggs and larvae of grasshoppers in a similar manner.

Nemognatha is a beetle that parasitizes leafcutting bees. These bees make egg cells lined with disks of leaf that they cut and carry to their nests. The beetle breaks open the cells, as the picture shows, and feasts on the developing larvae.

A group of small beetles (Rhiphiphoridae) with no common name is also parasitic on bees. They have an interesting life history and a strange appearance. Neither males nor females live more than a day as adults and they spend that time looking for one another. The females attract the males with an odor so that as soon as one emerges from its chamber in the nest of a host bee, the males find it and mate. The males emerge a little earlier and spend almost their entire short lives flying near the bees' nests, looking for females. After mating, the females immediately stop producing the attracting pheromone, and the males depart.

The female then looks for the flower preferred by the kind of bee which serves as host. She lays a large number of eggs, each of which hatches into an active little larva similar to that of the blister beetle. The larva attaches to a visiting bee and is carried back to the nest in much the same manner. Once in the nest it makes its way to a newly made cell in which a freshly laid bee egg sits with the food provided for it by the adult bees. The beetle larva waits for the much larger bee egg to hatch and then attacks the larva and somehow crawls right inside it. The bee larva continues to live and provide nourishment for the beetle larva, which grows until it is much larger than it was at the time it arrived in the bee nest. This growth is unusual since it occurs by stretching the flexible parts of the beetle's skin rather than by molting.

The much enlarged larva passes the winter, and sometimes several years, in a hibernating condition. When it becomes active again, it cuts its way out of the bee larva. It finally molts and starts eating voraciously. It molts several more times and eats different parts of its still living host-larva meal. The host larva is finally consumed after about two weeks, and the beetle forms a pupa which transforms into the short-lived adult. These small beetles have very short elytra. Their brief life as adults makes it difficult to find specimens, and their short elytra make them look less like beetles. Both of these factors combine to make these interesting beetles rare in collections.

Beetles that live at the expense of others are usually called parasites. But there is only one beetle known to live as a parasite of warm-blooded animals. This is a minute beetle which spends its entire life in the fur of the beaver and which probably feeds on the skin and fur of its host. A few related beetles (Leptinidae) are found in the nests of mammals such as mice, shrews, and moles. Another family from Australia (Aculognathidae) occurs in birds' nests, but none of these have actually become parasitic on the animals with which they live. It is possible, however, that these groups will provide the raw material for the future evolution of beetles parasitic on mammals and birds, one of the few major animal niches which beetles have thus far failed to occupy.

Nine

Beetle Friends and Foes

Despite their incredible numbers, beetles have not made the impact on the human imagination that more obvious but perhaps less significant animals have. We can hardly ignore the economic effects of beetles' lives, however— each year in the United States millions of dollars are lost by farmers and lumbermen due to beetle activities. But beetles can be friends to us as well as enemies, sometimes in surprising ways.

While the sacred scarab is by far the most important beetle in folklore, it is not the only one. The beetle is even more important to one South American tribe than the scarab was to the ancient Egyptians, for these people believe that a huge beetle was the creator of the world and made men and women from the left-over bits of dirt.

The large scarabs have also made their impact on human superstitions. The European dor beetle is associated with bad luck. It was the witch beetle to some Austrians, Germans, and Swiss, who said it knew the devil personally. Needless to say, the beetle was thought to have supernatural powers. If you killed it, a terrible storm would descend upon you. But on the other hand, if you rescued a dor beetle lying on its back, it could save you and your home from the elements.

The stag beetle was considered another insect villain. It was thought to set houses afire by carrying glowing coals to the roof in its huge jaws. It might also attract lightning. But if the head and jaws of a stag beetle were worn on a cap in France or Rumania, they could help fend off the evil eye.

The largest rove beetle in Britain also is considered akin to the devil; it is called the devil's coach horse or the devil's footman. This tough customer may be more than three centimeters (over an inch) long and is completely black. If disturbed, it raises its tail end and opens its big mandibles wide. It can release a nasty scent from glands beneath the tip of its abdomen. Small wonder that some Irish people, who called it the devil's beast, believed that it eats the bodies of dead sinners!

Helpful Beetles

While it is easy to catalogue the beetles which act as pests to humans, it is more difficult to identify precisely the "good guys." Often we discover to our dismay how useful a particular type of plant or animal was in the scheme of things after we have eliminated it or reduced its population drastically; the dung beetles in Australia are a perfect example. So much of the good that beetles do goes on silently and unnoticed. Ground beetles eat harmful insects and help keep their numbers under control. Dung beetles remove cow and horse dung and help keep pastures clean and free of flies and other pests.

Wood-boring beetles which attack dead wood help speed up the process of returning the organic substance of old logs to the earth where it can be used by plants for growth.

Scientists often use beetles as research animals. The mealworm beetle Tenebrio has been used in innumerable scientific studies dealing with insect development, chemical communication, and other aspects of insect life. Firefly luminescence has also been studied extensively as an example of the widespread and important phenomenon of bioluminescence. The chemical reaction producing light is used to detect the presence of the energy-carrying compound ATP. Very minute amounts of ATP can set off the firefly light system, which is therefore a sensitive assay for the presence of ATP.

One almost gruesome use to which beetles are put by scientists is the cleaning of skulls and other bones. Animal skulls are useful in various scientific studies such as those of growth patterns, dental decay, and species identification. It is a tricky and messy job to remove all the flesh from skulls by hand, but beetles of the family Dermestidae can do it with no trouble at all, and go easily into remote crevices. These scavengers eat everything but the hair and bone itself, leaving clean, white skulls and loose hair after only a few hours of voracious feeding.

Ladybird Beetles

One group of beetles which people have recognized as beneficial—and attractive—for a long time is the ladybird beetles, also called ladybugs, lady beetles, lady's beetles, and God's beetles (Coccinellidae). These hungry preda-

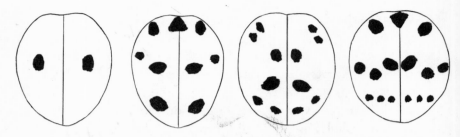

There are some 350 species of ladybird beetles with varied colors and markings. Left to right, the elytra of the two-spotted, nine-spotted, convergent, and fifteen-spotted.

tors eat tremendous numbers of scale insects and aphids each year, increasing immeasurably the value of farmers' and gardeners' crops and the beauty of people's gardens. Ladybirds have always been thought of as bringers of good fortune. The word "lady" in their name refers to the mother of Jesus, Mary, also called Our Lady. The exact reason for this association is not completely clear, but it may be traced to a legend. During a great insect infestation of the grain fields at some past time, the people prayed to Our Lady for help. Swarms of ladybird beetles came at that time and quickly brought the pests under control, saving the crops.

The familiar rhyme "Ladybird, ladybird, fly away home, your house is on fire, your children will burn" may be based on the custom of burning hops after the harvest. At this time, many ladybirds and their larvae would still be present on the plants. But since various versions of the rhyme are found in many European countries without an annual hop harvest, this explanation may be too simple. The actual origin may lie far deeper in the ancient associations of beetles and humans. Some believe that in the past there was some recognition of the relationship of the lady beetle with the scarabs; perhaps, they say, the beetles "house" is the sun, on fire at sunset.

Whatever the origin of the rhyme, the existence of the beetle is a blessing to us for sure. There are hundreds of lady beetle species scattered around the world. Most can be identified by the number of spots on their backs. One kind has only two, while another has as many as fifteen. The appetite of a lady beetle adult or larva for aphids is a joy to behold. One in California was seen to eat 475 aphids (an average of 25 each day). As an adult, it averaged 34 aphids a day. In addition to aphids and scale insects, lady beetles will eat mealybugs, white flies, and insect eggs. They are altogether handy creatures to have in one's garden or fields.

If one isn't fortunate enough to have a resident population of these useful insects, one can buy them in large quantities to release in the garden. They are collected by the gallon from their winter gathering places. Unfortunately, once they are released, one cannot force them to stay. While many people are convinced that their crops may be saved by a healthy dose of lady beetles at the right time, others complain that the insects won't stick around to do the job assigned to them but fly off to eat someone else's aphids.

Unpopular Beetles

Many of the farmer's greatest villains are beetles. The boll weevil is a prime example. When the southern states first grew cotton, there were no boll weevils there to damage their crops. Cotton made many southern farmers rich. Then, in the 1890s, the first boll weevils were seen in Texas. They had migrated up from Central America or Mexico and found a gold mine of cotton plants in our southern states. These beetles multiplied so fast that they spread northward at a rate of 60 miles a year until they inhabited almost the whole cotton-growing region of the South. Many farmers went bankrupt, and some banks were even forced to close.

In the United States alone, boll weevils cause about $200 million worth of crop losses each year, sometimes much more. Even today, with great spraying of cotton with DDT and other pesticides, the weevils may take over half the total southern cotton crop in a bad year. New ways of controlling these pests, such as deadly weevil diseases, are being tried out all the time. But we clearly have a long way to go before this destructive creature is under control.

One reason this insect is so successful is that it can undergo several generations during the long warm season in the South. The adult beetles overwinter in protected places—a trash heap will do. When it warms up, the beetles head for the nearest cotton field. The female beetle bores a neat hole into a cotton flower bud with her long snout. She puts one egg inside and goes on to another bud. The larva hatches in just three to five days and feeds for only a week or two. The pupal stage is only another three to five days. The new beetle cuts its way out and immediately begins to feed some more on the cotton buds, blossoms, and bolls (the bolls are the seed pods of the cotton plant). After only three or four days of adult feeding, the female weevil can begin to lay eggs. This rapid life cycle means that only three weeks pass from egg to egg-layer; seven generations can be produced in a year. When the food is unlimited as it is in big cotton fields, the beetles can multiply their numbers incredibly in one season, damaging the crops enormously. The feeding of the weevils may kill the cotton flower bud outright, or it may be damaged so that the bolls have very little usable cotton fiber when they mature.

A boll weevil punctures the hole in which she will deposit an egg.   DR. PHILIP S. CALLAHAN

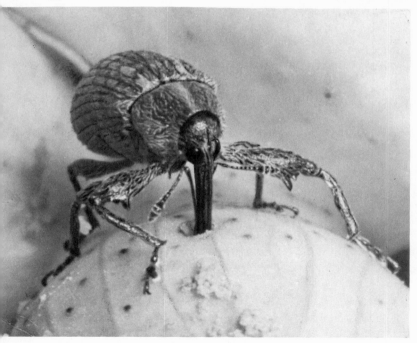

The Japanese Beetle

While the boll weevil eats a very limited type of food and thrives because of the human habit of planting huge fields all of one crop, the Japanese beetle is successful because of its varied food habits. This small, shiny green and copper pest can thrive on more than 275 different kinds of trees, shrubs, and small plants. When it first appeared in New Jersey in 1916, no one knew what it was. But within eight years it had become established over 2500 square miles, and people were worried about it. The beetle was traced to Japan, but even there little was known about it. It was not a dangerous pest in its homeland. The Japanese beetle was like the Klamath weed: introduced by accident into a new land where it had no enemies, it prospered and caused much economic damage. From 1922 to 1933, scientists searched Japan for potential enemies of the Japanese beetle which might be brought to this country to control it. They found a number of possible predators and parasites and chose a selection of more than 40 of the most promising to try out. These were found not only in Japan but also Australia and Hawaii.

Fortunately, two of the parasites have become well established in their new home and manage to make problems for the beetles. Both are very small wasps which lay their eggs on the beetle larvae. One beetle disease has also proved effective. This "milky disease" makes the beetle larva's blood appear milky and can kill.

The Colorado potato beetle, Leptinotarsa, decemlineata. *This handsome insect is a potent destroyer of potatoes, and also tomatoes, peppers, and other vegetables. Note the egg mass at upper left.*

The Colorado Potato Beetle

The Japanese beetle became such a dangerous pest in this country because it was introduced into a country where it lacked natural enemies. The Colorado potato beetle is a dangerous pest because the crop on which it feeds was introduced from somewhere else. This beetle was a native of the Rockies and fed on a native plant called buffalo burr, which is a relative of the potato. When settlers arrived at the eastern slope of the Rockies in the mid-nineteenth century, they brought potatoes with them. Plants in the potato family, including the tomato, eggplant, and deadly nightshade, contain poisons in their leaves, and very few insects can eat them. But the chemical composition of potato leaves was very much like that of the buffalo burr, and the Colorado potato beetles quickly adapted to feeding on the new food. They spread eastward, from potato field to potato field, wiping out entire crops. By 1874, they reached the Atlantic coast and had crossed the ocean into Germany by 1877.

One trait of the Colorado potato beetle makes it very hard to control. It stores up the poisonous chemicals from its food plant in its own body, making it unappetizing to birds and other potential predators. The adult beetle, with its striking black and yellow stripes, is quite conspicuous, as are the orange eggs and red larvae. But all are left alone by predators. The life cycle of this beetle is fast enough, too, that there may be more than one generation a season.

Bark Beetles

The bark beetles are interesting insects, but very serious economic pests. There are many kinds in the United States. Some trees which lose their leaves in winter are attacked by bark beetles, but few of them are economically important. The elm bark beetle carries Dutch elm disease, which can kill a big tree in only one season, and the hickory bark beetle found in the central states may cause a loss of $15 million in one year. But the most dam-

aging bark beetles are those which attack evergreen trees. Bark and ambrosia beetles destroy as much as four and a half thousand million board feet of timber each year. This translates into hundreds of millions of dollars worth of lumber. The beetles rarely seriously threaten a forest; they are part of the natural balance of nature in areas where they are found. But when people want wood to build their homes, the trees which have been attacked by the beetles may be too damaged to be useful. Thus, from the human point of view, these beetles are "dangerous." The reason we know so much about the interesting communication systems of bark beetles is because of their economic importance. If we can understand how they communicate with one another, perhaps we can interfere with that communication to prevent them from attacking trees. Laboratory scientists have, for example, produced a synthetic mixture of the three chemicals found in the elm bark beetle sex attractant. This mixture is every bit as attractive to male beetles as the real thing. If a way can be worked out to use this artificial attractant to lure male beetles in large enough numbers, we can be a step ahead in our efforts to control the beetles.

Other Economic Pests

The list of nuisance beetles goes on and on. There is the Mexican bean beetle, the "bad guy" of the ladybird beetle family. This pest eats bean leaves and pods instead of aphids and scale insects, but it is every bit as hardy and successful as its helpful cousins. In some areas, the Mexican bean beetle makes it just about impossible to raise a bean crop. Wireworms, which are the root-feeding larvae of click beetles, attack the roots of many crops, including wheat, corn, sugar beets, and potatoes. They are found naturally in grasslands. If the grass is plowed up and the land planted with crops, the wireworms are there to feast. There may be eight million of them in an acre of soil, enough to cause severe crop losses.

Beetles don't damage only growing plants. Flour beetles attack stored grains and ground flour, also causing millions of dollars of damage annually. Carpet beetle larvae eat through any sort of fiber, including telephone insulation and even synthetic fabrics. Clearly, the beetles are ahead right now in their competition with humans. Perhaps as we learn more about these highly successful creatures, we will find out how to control the dangerous ones and how to appreciate the helpful ones. But dangerous, helpful, or just plain existing, without any particular relationship with the human race, beetles are certainly among the most fascinating animals alive.

Ten

Observing and Collecting Beetles

One of the nice things about beetles is that besides reading about them, one can look at them to learn more. There are so many beetles that there is no reason why one cannot watch them and so learn something about what they eat and how they defend themselves. And by making a collection one learns to identify the types that live nearby. Watching live beetles will sharpen one's view of the world of nature and make one notice things not seen or realized before—especially if one constantly asks oneself questions. The hunt for beetles is a challenge, because one has to think about the things beetles like to eat and the places they are likely to be found.

Beetles of some sort may be found just about anywhere, and the inside of one's own home may provide a few types to begin with. Searching under rocks or old boards usually yields common beetles such as ground beetles if the soil is damp enough. Leaves and flowers also often provide a good selection of beetles such as ladybirds and leaf beetles. Certain types of beetles tend to occur together in groups, such as those usually found on goldenrod flowers in the eastern United States in the late summer.

An easy first project is to watch common ground beetles using their antenna cleaners on the front legs. Ground beetles are abundant and easy to find under stones in the garden or on a vacant lot. All of them have somewhat similar structures. Put the beetle into a light-colored container so it can be seen clearly. Blow some fine powder (white chalk dust or corn starch would show up well against a black ground beetle) and look for the beetle's reactions under a magnifying glass. Some of the larger ground beetles have to step on the end of the antenna to hold it in position for the antenna cleaner to be run along it. Others have deep grooves with built-in guiding hairs; species so equipped need not step on the antenna, since the groove itself will hold it in position. Most ground beetles use modified spines on the end of the middle tibia to clean the combs of the antenna cleaner. It has been suggested that other bristles on the ends of the front tibia are used in turn to clean the comb-cleaner. Can you find any evidence for such a complicated sequence of events? Do you see white powder accumulating in the antenna cleaner itself, or at the ends of either the middle or front tibiae?

Water beetles are also interesting to hunt and to watch. In this pursuit an aquarium net is very helpful, though not absolutely necessary. Some beetles can be caught by hand, and many more can be removed from masses of aquatic plants and debris after you have hauled them from the water. Different kinds of water beetles will be found in different habitats. Small temporary pools may have a few, but larger quiet ponds with lots of vegetation will contain many more. Different kinds may be found along the banks of large lakes, and still others in and on fast-moving streams.

A wide-mouth net is especially important for catching ʼirligig beetles, since they swim so rapidly and can detect the net as it comes at them. They may turn or dive, and the net opening must be large so that they cannot evade it. It takes a lot of luck and patience to catch whirligigs in a jar or other such small-mouthed container.

If you find a group of whirligig beetles, watch them for a while and see if they seem to come close to hitting one another. How do the beetles respond to your putting the net handle among them? Try to follow a single beetle through the crowd as it bobs and weaves and turns abruptly. If you can catch one, put it in a jar with some water to watch it swim. Does it hit the sides of the jar? Does it swim under water as well as on top? If so, does it swim faster under water or on the top?

Any time you find a beetle and can get close to it, watch what it is doing. Try to catch it and observe which escape mechanisms it uses. If you succeed in capturing it, hold it gently between your fingers and examine it closely. What sort of mouthparts, legs, and wings does it have? Does it have notches for withdrawing its legs and antennae when it drops from a plant? With the help of a magnifying glass and a paper cup or a jar to hold the beetle, one can learn a lot about beetles; how they are put together, and how they live.

Raising Beetles

An easy beetle to raise at home is the mealworm, which is really the larva of a darkling beetle (*Tenebrio molitor*). These larvae are often available in pet shops as food for lizards and toads. They may be kept in almost any container. Put in the feed, such as wheat bran or corn meal, to a depth of several inches and cover with a damp—not wet—piece of cloth. Then place an additional inch or so of food over the cloth and add the mealworms. If the container is shallow, it should be covered with wire mesh so the beetles cannot escape. The larvae should live and develop well with no further care than the weekly addition of a slice of potato for moisture. After the culture has grown for a while, it should be easy to find larvae of different sizes, pupae, and adults, and watch the accumulation of molted larval skins.

You can observe the behavior of your mealworms any time you like. If you can find larvae of darkling beetles in woods or fields (this is more likely if you live in the West), try raising them under similar conditions. Mealworms require very little water, and the weekly potato slice will supply them with enough. However, if you are working with an unknown species, it is better to sprinkle or spray a bit of water on the food every day or two to be sure the larvae have enough. Don't get the food so wet that mold starts to grow on it, though. If mold does appear, remove the moldy food and replace it with fresh, dry food; and be more careful with the spraying after that. If the potato slice gets moldy, remove it and don't put in a fresh slice for several days.

If you are keeping a beetle collection, you can attempt to collect and preserve the larval and pupal stages as well as the adults when they emerge, to get a complete sequence. Such collections, in which the larvae and adults are certainly of the same species, are most useful to entomologists, and they exist for only a small proportion of the beetles native to the United States.

It is also possible, with a bit of effort, to rear the larvae of water beetles, such as the larger hunting diving beetles (Dytiscidae). These saber-tooth larvae are found in the same waters in which the adults live. Spring is the best time to hunt for them. The process of development may be observed closely in water beetles since the larvae are active and may be kept in a specially arranged aquarium.

The aquarium may be as small as one or two gallons, but it should be prepared carefully as follows. Put a half-inch layer of stone chips (previously heated to sterilize them) in the dry tank. On top of this place an inch and a half of clean aquarium sand (also heat-sterilized). Then add a thick layer of very moist earth (not mud) at one end, about five inches deep and covering at least five inches of the surface. The earth should be collected from the side of the pond in which the larvae were captured. Mix in some old moss to break up the soil (small wood chips will do in the absence of moss). Along one side of the mass of moss and dirt, stand up three pieces of flat rock such as slate, about a quarter inch thick and about two inches by three inches in size. These will help stabilize the bank. There should be an inch and a half of space between the rocks to give the beetle larva a place to enter the earth bank when the time for pupation arrives.

Now add pond water gently to a depth of about two and a half inches, allowing the top of the mound to remain out of the water. This is very important. After the water has settled for a few hours, add a few sprigs of Elodea (the water plant sometimes sold as Anacharis in pet stores) and a maximum of two beetle larvae. If you put in more than two, they will eat one another. Keep the tank out of direct sunlight so that the water does not get too hot. The larvae should be fed tadpoles and small fish, of which seven or eight should be present in the aquarium at all times. The water should be removed once every four days and replaced with fresh pond water. Other aquatic insect larvae may be used as food if tadpoles or small fish are not available. Partially eaten food should also be removed.

When the larvae grow as big as they are going to (and this can be up to three inches long in large species), they get very restless and stop eating. Such larvae will shortly disappear from view if the aquarium is undisturbed. They burrow into the artificial bank and form pupal cells within the dirt, where they will transform into adult beetles. If the earth over the pupa is removed very carefully, the development of the pupa can be watched from day to day. The hole may be plugged with damp moss between observations. When the adults appear (after about two weeks) they can be maintained on the same diet for a while. However, they do not do as well as the larvae in aquaria.

Rearing larvae found in the field is quite easily done with wood-boring beetles, whose larvae inhabit branches and twigs. You will soon learn to recognize the small holes, the piles of sawdust, and the larval trails in the wood which indicate that there may be living larvae present. Cut the branches into strips of moderate length and take them home. Keep them in a closed box in a cool place, preferably outside or in a garage so that the temperatures are approximately those that occur in nature. If you insert a glass vial horizontally in a small hole in the box, emerging beetles will come to the light let in through the vial and will accumulate in it. You can thus check easily on the progress of your culture. This takes lots of patience, since many of these beetle larvae live for two years or longer, and they tend to emerge only at certain seasons. But in this way it is often possible to get specimens of species which are not easy to collect as adults in nature; and if you know what sort of wood you have put in the box, you know at least one kind of wood in which the beetle breeds. It is always exciting to check one of these rearing containers, since you never know what might turn up.

Collecting Equipment

If you decide to make a beetle collection, it would be best to do it well from the start. You can collect many beetles with no further equipment than your hands and a jar to put them in, but to really find out what lives out there, a few additional things are very helpful. The following is the basic equipment you will need to collect beetles:

1. *Killing jars with alcohol or ethyl acetate*
2. *Envelopes and a sturdy crushproof box to put them in*
3. *Pen and tape for labeling*
4. *Net (both sweeping and aerial if possible)*
5. *Small chisel, screwdriver, or crowbar*
6. *Forceps*
7. *An old sheet*

The following equipment is helpful in special situations:

1. *An aquarium net*
2. *A small shovel (portable folding type is best)*
3. *Bucket*

4. *Funnel and stand set up beneath a light bulb (Berlese funnel)*
5. *Pitfall traps*

The easiest killing material to obtain is rubbing alcohol. It will preserve the beetles quite well. Just drop them into a plastic jar half-filled with the alcohol. But beetles killed in alcohol tend to get stiff and difficult to mount, especially if you keep them in the fluid for a while. A better way is to use ethyl acetate, if you can get it. Beetles killed with ethyl acetate remain soft and are much easier to mount neatly. One uses the fumes of this chemical to kill the beetles. Moisten some facial tissue or toilet paper with a few drops of ethyl acetate and place it in the killing jar just before use. Then drop the beetles in.

Ethyl acetate is probably not available at your neighborhood drugstore. It can be bought from the biological supply houses which usually supply schools. Some supply houses will sell you equipment, but they will not usually sell chemicals to individuals. The best way to get ethyl acetate (and probably anything else) from such companies is to order through your school. Your science teacher will probably know how to do this and be willing to help. Ethyl acetate is not deadly to humans, but it is poisonous enough to be dangerous. You should not breathe it deeply or put your hands in it. It dissolves many kinds of plastic, so glass jars are necessary. These should be wrapped with electrical tape to minimize the danger of breakage on collecting trips.

If you collect in more than one place in a day it is important to have a number of collecting jars so that beetles from different locations or different situations (for example, a rotten cedar log or a stream bank) can be kept separate from one another. It is important that as much of this information as possible be put on the labels which are to go with the beetles so that when they are mounted, the information is not lost. Dead beetles should be removed from the killing jars and stored in envelopes (small glassine envelopes of the kind available for stamp collectors work very well). The collecting information, including at least the location (state, county, and city, or distance and direction from a city or town) and the date should be written on the envelope before the beetles are put in. Further data concerning plant host, time of day, activity in which the beetle was engaged, collecting method used, and so forth, are also quite valuable and should be recorded. The envelopes should then be sealed with tape and kept in a crushproof container like a cigar box or large can for the rest of the trip.

Many insect collectors have two kinds of nets. One is the same as a butterfly net, meant for catching flying insects. These are light nets made of a fine but transparent material through which you can see readily, and which do not catch the air in the bag. They are called aerial nets. The second type is heavier. It usually weighs more and is sturdier, meant for sweeping through leaves and grass, or for use in shaking the branches of trees and bushes from beneath, to catch whatever might fall. This type of net is probably more useful to a person interested in beetles, but aerial nets are often more readily available. Nets don't work well when they are wet, and unless you are collecting water beetles, they should be kept dry. You also have to be careful not to snag the net on thorns, cactus spines, and the like if you want to keep it in good condition.

There are directions for making your own net in the insect book by Borror, DeLong, and Triplehorn mentioned in the Suggested Reading list.

The aerial net is used for catching flying beetles. Warm, sunny spring afternoons are particularly rewarding. If you stand looking toward the sun with your eyes in the shadow of a tree, you will be able to see all sorts of insects in flight. Beetle flight is usually fairly slow and in a straight line. With experience, you will find yourself swinging mostly at beetles. Some that can be caught like this cannot be found on flowers and are generally difficult to find. The aerial net is particularly useful when searching for wood-boring beetles at a woodpile or in a lumber yard. The metallic wood-boring beetles especially may be found on freshly cut wood as they look for places to lay their eggs. They prefer very hot afternoons, and they tend to stay in the sun. These beetles, and others associated with wood, fly well, and when they are hot they are fast. You have to be fast, too, to catch one of these prizes on the wing. Lumber yards are best on weekends, when the yard is quiet.

The aerial net is also very important for catching tiger beetles, which must be stalked and caught individually. Tiger beetles spend most of their time on the ground, but they are usually found in the sun on sandy soil or on paths or trails. When they are warm, they take off very quickly if disturbed, fly a short distance close to the ground, and then land again. It is best to try to catch them on the ground by swinging the net down hard over them, so that when they try to take off they fly into the net. The best target area is smooth and without rocks or roots which will lift the side of the net and give the beetle a means of escape. Tiger beetles are very fast, and they often get away even after you have managed to get a net over them.

The excitement is not over when you get the tiger beetle in the net, since with their powerful jaws they can give you a memorable nip. By swinging the net hard through the air, you can force the beetle to the end. Then you have to quickly grab the net near the end to enclose the beetle in a little pocket at the tip. Then take off the cover of your killing jar with one hand and put it into the net so that the opening is just beneath the spot you are pinching together between your thumb and the side of your index finger. When the open jar is in place, set its base on the ground and open the little bag containing the beetle. Push the tip of the net quickly into the jar, keeping the opening tightly covered with the net. When you can see that the beetle is in the jar, well away from the mouth, *quickly* slip the cap of the jar in underneath the part of the net you have been holding over the mouth and seal the jar tightly. You can also try to grab the beetle's body through the net, which makes it much easier to put it into the jar, but you have to be sure to grab it along the sides and from the rear. Tiger beetles can bite right through the thin mesh of an aerial net.

To use the sweeping net, just push it quickly through the grass with a sweeping motion, and examine the contents of the net after a few sweeps. What you find will be interesting, although there may be no beetles present. Many other insects and spiders will also be captured by this method, some of which may startle you as they leap or fly from the net. The trouble with capturing beetles by sweeping is that you really don't know much about what the beetle was doing before you caught it—what sort of plant it was sitting on and whether it was feeding; whether there were a lot of them on one plant and few on the next or whether they are evenly distributed, and so on. And since many beetles drop to the ground when they are alarmed, many evade the net successfully.

A more informative technique is to spread a sheet or similar white cloth on the ground beneath a tree or bush and then to strike the trunk or major overhanging branches hard with a stick, causing beetles to drop to the ground. If you beat only one kind of tree or bush, you will know that what you catch must have been on it. The beetles will land on the sheet and you will easily be able to see them, after you learn to distinguish them from bits of debris that also fall. Remember, though, that many beetles will remain motionless for as long as five minutes after they drop, and that you often may not be sure what is a beetle until it begins to move. You must be patient to find all the beetles which you have beaten from their perch.

The chisel or crowbar will be especially useful when you are exploring a rotten log. It will help in prying off bark, in breaking up the rotten wood, in checking bracket fungi, and in turning over heavy objects. A tool such as a small crowbar is especially useful for turning over rocks and boards in places known to be inhabited by poisonous animals—spiders, scorpions, snakes, and such, which might also have taken refuge beneath the rock. Such a tool makes it unnecessary to risk putting your hands in a spot you have not yet been able to check.

The forceps are handy for all sorts of things, especially when you are trying to pick up small beetles.

Special Situations

The additional equipment listed is handy if you want to try to collect beetles from special situations. For instance, to find beetles which live among the moist twigs and dead leaves of a forest floor, collect leaves, twigs, bits of soil, and their associated molds and fungi. Bring all of this home in a container. Set up a large funnel (plastic is fine) supported so it stands up with the narrow end pointing down to empty into a small jar. Place a few handfuls of the leaf litter in the funnel and put a burning light bulb over the top of the funnel so that the litter dries out from the top. The beetles (and many other kinds of small animals) will move away from the light and over a period of hours will land in the jar beneath.

You can put alcohol in the jar and let the beetles land directly in it or capture the beetles alive for further observations. Most of these beetles will be very small, however, and a good magnifying glass will be useful to see what you have captured. More elaborate versions of this sort of apparatus are used by professional entomologists under the name of the Berlese funnel, after the Italian entomoogist who developed it.

It is also possible to sift leaf litter and such through a fairly coarse strainer onto a white cloth. (The mesh should preferably be about two millimeters or more; a fine-mesh tea strainer would let very little through.) In this case, however, all the fine particles come through in addition to the animals. The beetles must then be sorted from the rest of the debris. The forceps and a magnifying glass are very helpful in finding the beetles. This procedure has the advantage that it can be done in the field. It helps in checking whether any beetles are actually present in a given spot, and therefore whether it is worth bringing material home or not. The strainer is also useful for sifting the dirt under rotten logs. If the wood is really rotten, it too may be crushed with a hand over the strainer to see if any small beetles fall out.

Beetles may also be taken in traps and these may be used with or without bait. Simple pitfall traps are just cans set into the ground so that the edges are even with the soil. Beetles, especially ground beetles which are active at night, will fall into the trap as they wander around and they cannot get out again. If a funnel can be fitted into the can so that it is flush with the edge or fits just beneath it, the trapped insects can be collected in a small vessel which can be replaced easily. This helps to keep large pieces of debris and larger animals, such as mice and shrews, from falling into the trap.

Such traps must be attended to fairly frequently, if the beetles are to be captured alive. The beetles which fall in will often fight with one another, and they may mutilate and kill one another. Water also tends to collect in the traps after a rain or even a heavy dew. Traps may also be baited to attract specific kinds of insects, although many of the most successful baits are rather unpleasant. Dead animals or rotten meat, animal feces, or rotten fruit or vegetation may be tried. Turpentine is attractive to wood-loving insects such as the longhorn beetles, checker beetles, and bark beetles. Turpentine should be placed in a shallow pan a few feet above the ground and close to the landing surfaces, since the beetles will not land in the turpentine itself. Some strange things can be attractive to beetles. Large numbers of the pretty longhorn beetle Rosalia have been attracted to a paint shop in Northern California; another longhorn was found coming to old watermelon rinds in Arizona. The interesting reticulated beetle *Priacma serrata* (one of the most primitive known beetles) is attracted to diluted Clorox in the forests of the inland Northwest.

Although it is possible to collect dung beetles by turning over cow pads with a stick and picking up the beetles with your forceps, there is another method, slightly less unpleasant. An old bucket and a small shovel are required. Fill the bucket almost to the top with water and then, with the shovel, carefully pick up a cow pad in which you have already seen beetles. Place it gently into the bucket. The beetles will be forced to leave the pad and come to the surface of the water where they are easily collected with a small aquarium net. (Don't plan to use the net for fish too.)

Preparing Your Specimens

For your collection at home, beetles should be mounted on insect pins and kept in suitable boxes where they will be pinned above a cork or polyethylene foam bottom. It is important to use specially made insect pins because they are longer than the straight pins used for sewing, they are narrower and do much less damage to the beetle, and they will not rust from moisture within the beetle. Insect pins may be obtained from some of the supply houses listed at the end of this book.

Beetles killed in alcohol may be kept in this solution

until they are pinned, and they may be pinned without further preparation. Beetles killed with ethyl acetate and stored in envelopes, however, may dry out and become brittle if they are not pinned within a few days. These must be "relaxed" before they can be pinned. A relaxing jar can be made from a wide-mouth gallon jar such as restaurants often receive mayonnaise or pickles in. In the bottom, place a layer of paper towels wetted with water so that they are moist but not dripping wet. Put some moth crystals (naphthalene, or for fuller protection, para-dichlorobenzene) in at this level, too. Then insert a piece of plastic foam or some other water-repellent surface to keep the envelopes containing the beetles from touching the damp towels. When the jar is tightly covered, the humidity inside stays high, and most beetles will relax within a day, except for the largest specimens, which should be allowed two days.

When pinning a beetle, insert the pin through the right elytron in such a way that it does not interfere with the legs below. It is usually inserted about one-third of the way down the elytron from the thorax. Some collectors like to arrange the legs and antennae of their specimens so that each pair is in approximately the same position. Although specimens prepared this way look nice when pinned in a row, it is better if the legs and antennae on each side are in slightly different positions. Then, if a leg covers an important structure needed to identify the beetle on one side, it can be seen on the other side. Enough room should be left on the pin above the beetle to make it easy to pick up the pin and move it without touching the beetle. Pinned beetles may get very dry and brittle and they are

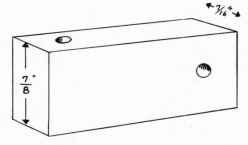

This little wood block is helpful in mounting insects.

easily damaged once they have been in the collection for a while.

Beetles are mounted at a standard height of ⅞ inches from the bottom of the pin. As a guide it will be helpful to prepare a small block of wood with the dimensions shown in the picture, and two small holes drilled in it. When you have pushed the pin partly through the beetle, insert the point in the proper hole and continue pushing; this moves the beetle to the standard height on its pin. Then remove the pin from the block and stick it slightly into a data label showing where the beetle was collected and other information. Such labels are mounted on the pin ⁷⁄₁₆ of an inch from the bottom. Flip the block and push the pin through the proper hole so the label rises on the pin to ⁷⁄₁₆ of an inch.

A data label should be as small as possible, and is best arranged like this:

WASH. Whitman Co.
4 mi E Pullman
Jun 16, 78
P. Schroeder, Coll.
Feeding on rose

An additional label with biological data can be made and placed below the primary label if there isn't room on the top one for all the biological information you have.

Insect pins are available in various diameters from very thin (#ooo) to very heavy (#5). The most practical pins to use are #o, #1, #2, and #3. If a beetle is too small to pin on a #o pin, it should instead be mounted on a small "point" cut out of an index card or a similar card. Points should be in the form of an isoceles triangle with two seven-millimeter sides and a base two millimeters wide. A #2 pin is placed through the base, and the point is raised to the standard ⅞ inch level on the pin with the wooden block. The tip of the triangle is then bent down a bit so that the beetle may be attached by one side and a bit of its underside. The beetle is placed upside down on a block, the point is touched to a drop of white glue (such as Elmer's) and then to the insect in such a way that the insect will face away from you when it extends to the left of the pin. Only a *minute* bit of glue should be used to avoid smearing it all over the beetle.

Your collection may be kept in cigar boxes or something similar, with thin sheets of polyethylene foam or cork cut out to match the shape of the interior of the box and glued in to make a pinning bottom. As your collection grows, you may want to purchase some ready-made boxes for the collection. A number of different types are available from some of the supply houses. It will be necessary to beware of the insect collection's greatest enemy—live beetles! Carpet and museum beetles (Dermestidae) are found in many homes, and the larvae of these beetles seem to be able to eat almost anything. One of the authors once found a can of cayenne pepper in the kitchen full of the hairy larvae of these beetles, and they will also eat dead, dry insects such as the beetles in a collection. To guard against dermestids, the collection should be kept in boxes with tight-fitting lids; it is this requirement that makes commercially made insect boxes somewhat expensive. It is also necessary to keep some moth crystals in each box. The moth crystals last longer in boxes with tight-fitting covers, but they must be replaced periodically.

Once your beetles have been properly mounted and placed in an appropriate box, you will want to find out what they are. To do this, you will need to know a bit more about beetles than can be found in this book. Following this chapter is a Suggested Reading list of books, including some useful for beetle identification. You should choose one that is appropriate for the area you live in; and if possible, it is a good idea to have two of them available. Comparison of the two will help you to be surer of your decisions as to species. You will have to learn additional words for the parts of beetles which are used in the books, but once you have determined what kind of beetles you have, you will have learned what sorts of things to look for. Once you know what species your beetles are, you will have a better idea of what they should be doing the next time you encounter them. You will also find it helpful to be able to identify the common flowers, bushes, and trees and their parts in your area so that you can describe more fully where the beetles are and what they are doing as you observe them.

Biological-Supply Houses

ANN ARBOR BIOLOGICAL CENTER, INC.
6780 Jackson Rd.
Ann Arbor, Mich. 48103

BIOQUIP PRODUCTS
P.O. Box 61
Santa Monica, Calif. 90406

CAROLINA BIOLOGICAL SUPPLY CO.
Burlington, N.C. 27216

   Western address:
CAROLINA BIOLOGICAL SUPPLY CO.
Powell Laboratories
Gladstone, Oregon 97027

TURTOX/CAMBOSCO
8200 South Hoyne Ave.
Chicago, Ill. 60620

Glossary

aedeagus: Organ of male beetle used to place sperms inside the body of the female.

bark beetle: Member of the family Scolytidae, which consists of small beetles which bore into trees and lay their eggs there.

chitin: The tough material which makes up most of the insect exoskeleton.

chorion: The tough outer covering of the insect egg.

click beetle: Member of the family Elateridae, which consists of long, thin beetles which make a clicking sound.

cuticle: The outer nonliving layer of the insect body.

darkling beetle: Member of the family Tenebrionidae, which consists of many beetles most of which are scavengers. The familiar mealworm is the larva of a darkling beetle.

diving beetle: Diving beetles belong to the family Dytiscidae. Their hind legs are modified for swimming, and both adults and larvae are efficient hunters.

elytra: (singular: *elytron*) The hardened front wings of beetles, which are held over the functional second pair of wings.

firefly: Member of the family Lampyridae, which consists of beetles with glowing "lanterns" on the abdomen.

149

glowworm: Larvae or wingless, larvalike fem of
the families Lampyridae and Phengodidae, which

ground beetle: Member of the family Carabidae, which consists of hunting beetles which live on the ground.

ladybird beetle: Member of the family Coccinellidae, which
consists of small, brightly colored beetles most of which
feed on aphids and scale insects.

leaf beetle: Member of the family which consists of usually
brightly colored beetles which feed on leaves as both
larvae and adults.

longhorn beetle: Member of the family Cerambycidae, which
consists of beetles with especially long antennae and
which feed largely on plants.

luciferase: The enzyme present in the light organs of fireflies
which catalyzes the light-producing reaction.

luciferin: The chemical in fireflies that is stimulated by luciferase to produce light.

Malpighian tubules: A group of small tubes in insect bodies that
help eliminate wastes.

mandibles: The jaws of insects.

micropyle: A minute hole in the chorion of the insect egg
through which the sperms can pass to fertilize the egg.

molting: The process of shedding the old exoskeleton so that
the insect can grow; also called ecdysis.

peritrophic membrane: Membrane produced by special cells
in the insect intestine and which surrounds the mass of
food as it is digested.

pheromone: A chemical released by an animal which acts as a
message to another animal of its kind. Pheromones are
used to communicate alarm, attraction, and other things.

plastron: A film of air lying against an aquatic insect.

pronotum: The top of the prothorax.

prothorax: The first segment of the thorax, which bears the first pair of legs.

rove beetle: Member of the family Staphylinidae, which consists of beetles with short elytra. They live in many places and a large number are found in ant or termite colonies.

scarab beetle: Member of the family Scarabaeidae, which consists of small to very large, powerful beetles. The Hercules beetle, the Japanese beetle, and the dung beetles are all scarabs.

spiracle: The opening which lets air into the insect tracheal system.

tiger beetle: Member of the family Cicindelidae, which consists of large-eyed, brightly colored and fast-moving hunters.

tracheae: The air tubes which bring oxygen into the insect body.

weevil: Member of the family Curculionidae, which consists of beetles with bent antennae and a long snout. Many weevils are serious crop pests.

wireworm: The larva of a click beetle. Wireworms feed on roots and can seriously damage such plants as grass and strawberries.

Suggested Reading

Books

Arnett, Ross H., Jr., *The Beetles of the United States*. The American Entomological Institute, Ann Arbor, Mich., 1973. This manual for identification includes keys to almost all the known genera of American beetles. Its use requires knowledge of entomological terminology, but it is the best book available for the area. Not extensively illustrated.

Borror, D. J., D. M. DeLong and C. A. Triplehorn, *An Introduction to the Study of Insects*. Holt, Rinehart & Winston, N.Y., 4th ed., 1976. A college-level text of high quality.

Borror, Donald J., and Richard E. White, *A Field Guide to the Insects of America North of Mexico*. Houghton Mifflin Co., Boston, 1970. Contains a practical key to the families of beetles and illustrations of most of the important types. Well illustrated and relatively inexpensive.

Callahan, Philip S., *Insects and How They Function*. Holiday House, N.Y., 1971. Much information and unusual electron-microscope pictures.

———, *Insect Behavior*. Four Winds Press, N.Y., 1970. Also very informative; includes beetles and others.

Dillon, Elizabeth S., and Lawrence S. Dillon, *A Manual of*

Common Beetles of Eastern North America. Row, Peterson & Co., Evanston, Ill., 1961; also Dover, N.Y. (paperback). Probably the best bet as a starting book for those who live in this area.

Hatch, M. H., *The Beetles of the Pacific Northwest*. In five parts. University of Washington Press, Seattle, 1953–1971. An immense detailed work with many illustrations. Meant for the professional, so the keys may be difficult to use.

Jacques, H. E., *How To Know the Beetles*. Wm. C. Brown & Co., Dubuque, Iowa, 1951. Relatively inexpensive and limited in coverage, but contains a surprising number of illustrations and amount of information. Worthwhile even though somewhat out of date.

Wigglesworth, V. B., *Insect Physiology*. Halsted Press, N.Y. (Methuen Science Paperbacks), 7th ed., 1974. For those seriously interested in insects; by a world-famous researcher.

Magazine Articles

S. F. Arno, "Ladybug: Intrepid Mountaineer," *National Parks*, Sept. 1968

N. Barrie, "Like Knights of Old: European Stag Beetles," *International Wildlife*, Nov. 1974

J. Buck and E. Buck, "Synchronous Fireflies," *Scientific American*, May 1976

T. E. Eisner, "Beetle's Spray Discourages Predators," *Natural History*, Feb. 1966

M. Emsley, "Nature's Most Successful Design May Be Beetles," *Smithsonian*, Dec. 1975

H. E. Evans, "In Defense of Magic: the Story of Fireflies," *Natural History*, Nov. 1968

F. Graham, "Plague of the Pests: Control of the Cereal Leaf Beetle by the Anaphes Wasp," *Aubudon*, Sept. 1975

J. L. Gressitt, "Symbiosis Runs Wild on the Backs of High-Living Weevils," *Smithsonian*, Feb. 1977

G. Helgeland, "Flying Tiger with a Bite," *National Wildlife*, Feb. 1973

B. Hölldobler, "Communication Between Ants and Their Guests," *Scientific American*, March 1971

J. E. Lloyd, "Flashes and Behavior of Some American Fireflies," *Conservationist*, June 1969

L. J. Milne, "Social Behavior of Burying Beetles," *Scientific American*, Aug. 1976

E. B. Smith, "Nature's Leading Ladies," *National Wildlife*, Oct. 1968

L. A. Swan, "Pest-eating Insects," *National Wildlife*, Sept. 1964

E. Tanson, "This Pesticide Has Polka Dots," *National Wildlife*, April 1972

D. L. Tiemann, "Nature's Toy Train, the Railroad Worm," *National Geographic*, July 1970

D. F. Waterhouse, "Biological Control of Dung," *Scientific American*, April 1974

Index